BIRD SONGS

Recorded by the author and her husband

An album of long-playing records:
   BIRD SONGS OF DOORYARD, FIELD AND FOREST,
   Vol. I, Vol. II, Vol. III

BIRD SONGS

ADVENTURES AND TECHNIQUES IN
RECORDING THE SONGS OF
AMERICAN BIRDS

Norma Stillwell

INTRODUCTION BY DR. PETER PAUL KELLOGG

Garden City, New York
DOUBLEDAY & COMPANY, INC.
1964

To the memory of Jerry Stillwell
whose travel notes supplied
an important part of this book

CONTENTS

ILLUSTRATIONS

(all photographs by the author or her husband except as noted)

ix

ILLUSTRATIONS

INTRODUCTION

BASICALLY, Jerry Stillwell had the soul of an artist. He was one of the most energetic personalities I have ever known. Of Norma Stillwell, I'm not so sure, but I suspect that, in addition to being much like Jerry, she was a fountainhead of inspiration for a team, the team of Jerry and Norma Stillwell.

Though birds and the songs of birds perhaps became most important to them, they were both good naturalists. Norma's knowledge of botany combined with her keen observations and accurate descriptions are one of the many charms of this book. This with her soft sense of humor, wit, and intimate touches, her pat characterizations of birds and bees and beasts, and what they seemed to be saying when transposed to our language, make for easy reading and many will enjoy the suggestions for remembering the voices she tells about.

One of the Stillwell hobbies was combining the avian sounds they heard out of doors with music or poetry or prose and their sure knowledge of bird song plus a deep interest in the other arts endowed these efforts with a sense of beauty and feeling. I regret that more of this aesthetic depth could not be carried into the printed page, but it is much in evidence in their published discs.

While this book is in no sense a biography of Jerry Stillwell, it is a revelation of his character and this appears throughout in the author's depiction of so many light, telling incidents.

You admire Jerry's restless energy, which got him up long before the sun almost every morning. You sense his reverence for all nature and that he was a conservationist in the truest sense of the word.

Through the busy years of their life they had always maintained an active interest in birds and, with Jerry's retirement, they turned their attention to a relatively new phase of bird study—the recording of bird songs, primarily so that other people could hear them and thus become interested.

In all of us there is a bit of the missionary spirit. Both Jerry and Norma felt that they had a mission to perform. Perhaps "mission" and "perform" are not the right words, but when I first met them in southern Florida in 1950, it seemed that they felt they had discovered something so wonderful that they wanted to share it; call it what you will.

As a rule, artists have little time for technology and the scientific brick walls which bound their enthusiasms, but Jerry had experienced enough heartbreaks in his earlier recording efforts to know that there was a need for an understanding of the language of electrical engineering and for some of hard facts too. As you will guess from reading chapter IV, he was or became an apt pupil of the art of recording.

Coming into a field of scientific study from the business world, I have always suspected that Jerry was at first a bit suspicious of what Cornell's Laboratory of Ornithology had to offer or, to use Norma's words, "just what the pitch was." Actually this dedicated team of Jerry and Norma Stillwell was just what we of the Laboratory of Ornithology are always looking for—and only occasionally finding. One statement of the purpose of Cornell's Laboratory of Ornithology is: "To offer inspiration, encouragement and assistance to all who would study living birds, and recognition to those who achieve success." From this point of view, the Stillwells were definitely "our meat" and it was a challenge to help them and to share with them any knowledge we had picked up in the field of acoustical studies during the preceding twenty years of our work at Cornell.

During the weeks the Stillwells were with us during our sabbatic year, at first in our outdoor laboratory under southern Florida's palms, we fought the problems of "residual hum" to which Norma refers. Jerry took to the experiments like a duck to water. Early mornings found us in the field recording, and after lunch, for days on end, we would pull the equipment apart and spread it over tables in the yard behind our abode, testing and experimenting. It was a happy and fruitful experience for all the Kelloggs and the Stillwells and one we shall always remember with pleasure. And for Jerry it represented the beginning of a new phase of his recording experience and success. Apt and discerning and dedicated he was, and he responded not only to the demonstrated needs for new and more advanced technical equipment (though it was of real economic consideration at the time) but to the new and more arduous field techniques developed for use in recording biological sounds.

This book will appeal to many because it is the story of a hobby which ended in success—the success so many dream of for their hobby. While most of us don't say so, I believe that every amateur, and especially those who go in for bird study, hope to be able to eventually make some contribution, however modest, to the knowledge of the bird world. The Stillwells have done this. Their collection of the voices of over three hundred species of birds with varied selections from many parts of the birds' geographic range is a real contribution to science and education. From their work, twelve years of recording North American birds, several long-playing records of high educational value have been published. The entire Stillwell collection is now housed in Cornell's Library of

Natural Sounds, where it is available to scholars throughout the world for scientific study.

May this book be, and I believe it will be, an inspiration to lovers of birds everywhere. In so many places it makes one say, "I'd like to do something useful like that" and I hope you will have your wish.

PETER PAUL KELLOGG
Professor of Ornithology and Biological Acoustics
Cornell University, Ithaca, New York

31 Dec. 1963

AUTHOR'S NOTE

The fifth edition of the *Checklist of North American Birds* was published by the American Ornithologists' Union (AOU) in 1957, after our bird song records had been published. In addition to other changes in the fifth edition, all common names of subspecies were dropped even when differences in plumages, or songs, or both, are easily recognized in the field. In this non-technical book about our recording experiences, however, I have continued to use, in most places, the common names which were used on our records. The list below shows the changes in common names of birds represented on our three long-playing records: BIRD SONGS OF DOORYARD, FIELD AND FOREST.

AOU *Checklist*

Before fifth edition	*After fifth edition*
Arizona cardinal	cardinal
California purple finch	purple finch
alder flycatcher	Trail's flycatcher
Derby flycatcher	kiskadee flycatcher
Arkansas goldfinch	lesser goldfinch
green-backed goldfinch	lesser goldfinch
great-tailed grackle	boat-tailed grackle
California jay	scrub jay
Mearns's quail	harlequin quail
valley quail	California quail
Gambel's sparrow	white-crowned sparrow
Nuttall's sparrow	white-crowned sparrow
Puget Sound sparrow	white-crowned sparrow
desert sparrow	black-throated sparrow
western fox sparrow	fox sparrow

AUTHOR'S NOTE

Before fifth edition	*After fifth edition*
pinewoods sparrow	Bachman's sparrow
olive-backed thrush	Swainson's thrush
canyon towhee	brown towhee
red-eyed towhee	rufous-sided towhee
spotted towhee	rufous-sided towhee
blue-headed vireo	solitary vireo
western warbling vireo	warbling vireo
lutescent warbler	orange-crowned warbler
pileolated warbler	Wilson's warbler
Maryland yellowthroat	yellowthroat

For careful reading of my manuscript and many helpful suggestions, I am especially grateful to Dr. W. J. Baerg, Dr. Olin Sewall Pettingill, Jr., and Mrs. Ruth Rusch.

MAP KEY

Some favorite areas and birds recorded there are indicated by the numbers on the map endpapers of this book. They were selected from 1698 successful tape recordings of over 250 species, made during twelve years and 180,000 miles of travel. Those birds marked with a star (*) are pictured on the map near their numbered locations.

OREGON

1. CORVALLIS, lazuli bunting
2. BEND, fox sparrow
3. BURNS, sage thrasher*
4. CRATER LAKE, Cassin's finch
5. KLAMATH LAKE, black-headed grosbeak

WASHINGTON

6. ROSARIO BEACH, Puget Sound white-crowned sparrow
7. BAKER LAKE, varied thrush
8. MOUNT RAINIER, varied thrush
9. CHENEY LAKE REFUGE, common snipe, long-billed marsh wren
10. OLYMPICS, band-tailed pigeon*

UTAH

11. ZION NATIONAL PARK, western warbling vireo

IDAHO

12. CITY OF ROCKS, Brewer's sparrow

NEVADA

13. LAKE TAHOE, western warbling vireo, pileolated warbler

WYOMING

14. GRAND TETONS, green tailed towhee*
15. LUSK, McCown's & chestnut-collared longspurs

CALIFORNIA

16. POINT LOBOS STATE PARK, Nuttall's white-crowned sparrow
17. YOSEMITE, western fox sparrow
18. VENTURA, California purple finch
19. LOS ANGELES, California thrasher, wren tit
20. BIG BEAR LAKE, western fox sparrow, western tanager, Audubon's warbler*
21. MILL CREEK CANYON, mountain chickadee
22. BANNING, Lawrence's goldfinch, black-chinned sparrow

ARIZONA

23. ORGAN PIPE CACTUS NATIONAL MONUMENT, crissal thrasher
24. MESA, phainopepla, Bendire's thrasher
25. TUCSON, curve-billed thrasher, hooded orioles, Scott's orioles
26. MADERA CANYON, Steller's jay, acorn woodpecker*

xvii

27. PATAGONIA, Mearns's quail, crissal thrasher
28. TOMBSTONE, scaled quail, black-throated sparrow
29. CAVE CANYON, painted redstart, bridled titmouse
30. GRAND CANYON, hermit thrush

COLORADO

31. GARDEN OF THE GODS, magpie*
32. LIMON, lark bunting, horned lark
33. WALSENBERG, Arkansas goldfinch

NEW MEXICO

34. TRES RITOS, ruby-crowned kinglet
35. TAOS, Audubon's warbler
36. PECOS, pine siskin*
37. CARLSBAD, blue grosbeak

TEXAS

38. PALO DURO CANYON, scissortail
39. FORT DAVIS, canyon wren, house finch
40. BIG BEND NATIONAL PARK, vermilion flycatcher
41. CARRIZO SPRINGS, Bewick's wren*
42. HARLINGEN & "THE VALLEY," chachalaca, doves
43. KERRVILLE, Arkansas goldfinch
44. BEAUMONT, "BIG THICKET," hooded warbler, white-eyed vireo
45. TYLER, fox sparrow
46. DALLAS, painted bunting, Cassin's sparrow, black-capped vireo

OKLAHOMA

47. PAWHUSKA, prairie chicken*

KANSAS

48. BELVEDERE, DODGE CITY, western meadowlark
49. LAKE CITY, eastern meadowlark
50. ERIE, cardinal

LOUISIANA

51. LAKE CHARLES, redwing

MISSOURI

52. BIG SPRING STATE PARK, summer tanager

ARKANSAS

53. FAYETTEVILLE, "AVIAN ECHOES," bluebird, goldfinch, yellow-breasted chat*

ALABAMA

54. TUSCALOOSA, redstart

MISSISSIPPI

55. VICKSBURG, mockingbird

NORTH DAKOTA

56. DEVIL'S LAKE, marbled godwit,* clay-colored sparrow

SOUTH DAKOTA

57. BLACK HILLS, western meadowlarks

NEBRASKA

58. PLATTE RIVER, sandhill cranes,* tree sparrow
59. VALENTINE, yellow-headed blackbirds

MINNESOTA

60. THIEF RIVER FALLS, Franklin's gulls
61. ITASKA STATE PARK, common loons,* Baltimore orioles

MICHIGAN

62. CADILLAC, song sparrow
63. WARREN WOODS, wood thrush. towhee*

WISCONSIN

64. PARK FALLS, white-throated sparrow

IOWA

65. SPIRIT LAKE, upland plover

ILLINOIS

66. BLOOMINGTON, robin

INDIANA

67. MICHIGAN CITY, song sparrow

OHIO

68. CLEVELAND, pewee

VERMONT

69. RUTLAND BOG, swamp sparrow
70. MOUNT MANSFIELD, gray-cheeked thrush

NEW YORK

71. ADIRONDACKS, hermit thrush, purple finch, winter wren
72. ITHACA, Louisiana water-thrush
73. ALLEGHENY PARK, alder flycatcher

PENNSYLVANIA

74. POCONO LAKE, hermit thrush
75. WYALUSING, killdeer*

MAINE

76. ARCADIA NATIONAL PARK

MASSACHUSETTS

77. PLYMOUTH, Baltimore oriole*

CONNECTICUT

78. OLD GREENWICH, redwing, song sparrow

MARYLAND

79. SWALLOW FALLS, wood thrush, black-throated green warbler, veery, ovenbird

VIRGINIA

80. MOUNTAIN LAKE, rose-breasted grosbeak, chestnut-sided warbler, Canada warbler
81. LEXINGTON, cerulean warbler, prairie warbler
82. WARM SPRINGS, vesper sparrow
83. NICHOL'S PARK

WEST VIRGINIA

84. TERRA ALTA, bobolinks, yellow warbler
85. DURBIN, song sparrow

KENTUCKY

86. LOUISVILLE, Otter Creek Park, whippoorwill, cardinal,* Kentucky warbler, indigo bunting

NORTH CAROLINA

87. NEW BERN, laughing gull*

GEORGIA

88. THOMASVILLE, mockingbird, towhee, barred owl*
89. WAYCROSS, brown-headed nuthatch
90. ST. SIMON'S ISLAND, greater yellowlegs

FLORIDA

91. WAKULLA SPRINGS, limpkins*
92. EVERGLADES, purple gallinule, coots, herons, etc.
93. CYPRESS GARDENS, white-eyed towhee
94. SEBRING, ARCHBOLD BIOLOGICAL STATION, scrub jay
95. TAMPA, bobwhites, bald eagle*

BIRD SONGS

Chapter I

REEL BEGINNINGS

No wonder Jerry Stillwell's retirement hobby had something to do with birds. Ever since he was big enough to follow his father on holiday rambles through the woods, Jerry had been a bird watcher, and listener. His father was a just and gentle judge, a disciple of Thoreau and Burroughs. He encouraged the interests of his son through their outdoor experiences together and through an extensive library of nature books. A cabin on the bluff called Indian Hill, overlooking the Neosho River in southeastern Kansas, became the focal point of their nature and camping adventures. The judge was wont to approach the camp circle bringing a leafy twig or wild flower and thunder the command: "Class in natural history, stand up! Name this specimen." Not only was Jerry learning the flora, but, during his summer jobs as a grocer's delivery boy, he soon found every robin's nest in the little town of Erie.

I grew up under a mulberry tree, whose fruits are doubtless the best natural lure for the greatest variety of birds. Not until I met Jerry, as a classmate at the university in Lawrence, did I begin to realize there are many kinds of birds in addition to robins, redbirds, and "Jenny-wrens."

When Jerry first visited my home in Burlingame, my mother half suspected him of inventing some of the birds he claimed to have seen in our yard. "What would a Carolina

1

wren be doing in Kansas?" And, "Is a tufted titmouse really a bird?"

After our honeymoon Jerry began telling friends that, soon after meeting him, I had thrown away my violin and bought a bird book. I gave away my violin *after* he had given me the bird book. For thirty years we spent our holidays sauntering through the woods, mostly in Oklahoma and Texas. Our nature lore was absorbed from Nature herself. There were many good books, and better ones as the years passed. It was a long look-and-listen from Reed's *Pocket Bird Guide* to Peterson's field guides, Saunders' *Guide to Bird Songs*, and finally, just when we needed them most, Pettingill's two guides to bird finding.

Nature lore was only an absorbing hobby with us. Various congenial couples shared our casual nature excursions. In time we began sharing with the public our interest in birds and trees and wild flowers through a Sunday column in the Dallas *News* and through counseling such groups as Girl Scouts, Boy Scouts, and Camp Fire Girls.

We had come to Dallas in 1926 when Jerry began his work as technical editor for the American Petroleum Institute, which had just begun formulating specifications governing equipment used in the oil industry. As the number of published specifications and their revisions grew and spread into worldwide use, his editorial duties became so heavy and Jerry so engrossed with them that, since 1941, he had refused to take a vacation. I began to call him "Atlas." Yet, once he got the oil industry off his shoulders, Jerry would be needing a new world to carry. He was one of William Allen White's "eager souls." Fishing or lying in a hammock would never suffice for him.

Jerry was in high spirits the day his new Brush recorder arrived, March 20, 1948. It was the first moderately priced, portable tape recorder on the market. Now, he thought, he could record all the *good* music from radio and play it back whenever he liked. He was tired of jumping up every few minutes to change phonograph records. A reel of tape would play for half an hour; the seven and one-half inch per second speed was fast enough for good musical quality. Whenever he tired of a selection he could automatically erase it as he recorded a new one. At first he had expected the recorder to occupy only occasional leisurely hours. But merely recording radio music was not going to be enough to keep him occupied and happy after his retirement, which, we knew, must come soon. Little did he realize, when he wrote to his sister Rena to thank her for recommending the recorder, how far this ingenious little box would lead him.

Jerry came home from the office on March 31 and announced, casually, that he was forever through with derricks, cables, and walking beams, with tool-joints, couplings, and line pipe; that he had written his last "plug," his last "pitch," his "last scratch" for the API.

"Good for you, Jerry!" I tried to match his nonchalance in spite of an inward premonition that I had a piece of news to top his. "By the way, play back that bit of tape I recorded this morning."

Faint, indeed, but on the tape we heard *the song of a cardinal!* I had placed the microphone on the study window sill while the bird sang from the back fence, a hundred feet away. No wonder the song was faint! There flashed in both our minds the dream of a new hobby: recording bird songs on tape. We did not yet foresee how the dream would grow and lead us to spend the next twelve years tirelessly exploring the byways of every state between Canada and Mexico.

Our first successful recording, a half minute of song from the same cardinal which first enticed us into the project, was taped only a week after the first attempt. We had already begun to learn that recording the songs of wild birds would re-

3

quire many modifications of our equipment. Realizing that it would be necessary to get the microphone closer to the bird, we made the mistake of buying 100 feet of single-conductor cable to extend the microphone; this made the signal much too weak. After consulting an electronics expert, Jerry bought a low-impedance, dynamic microphone to replace (for long-distance use) the first one, a crystal-type. Since two-conductor cable was now required, the first long one had to be discarded. Then came a low- to high-impedance transformer to adapt the output of our new microphone to the recorder. Our bird recording had taken its first steps.

After Jerry had mounted the transformer inside the recorder case, to facilitate shifting between the two types of microphones, a strange hum was added to the recordings. He experimented for two days, then removed the transformer from the case and put it on the floor, two feet away. The hum disappeared.

Before daybreak one morning Jerry carried the Brush recorder into the garage and hung the microphone in a small tree just outside. He got a whisper song from a Carolina wren, more varied and continuous as well as softer than the typical song. Then came the sibilant call notes of a brown thrasher, and the barking of a fox squirrel. Background accompaniment grew intrusive, from barking dogs, roaring airplanes, hammering carpenters, and rattling milk trucks. City noises were encroaching ever closer onto our suburban acre.

Soon migrant thrushes began singing in R. A. Gilliam's ravine. Although his beautiful, twenty-acre sanctuary was in the heart of Oak Cliff, on the west side of the Trinity River in Dallas, the tree-shrouded slopes might help to screen out city noises. It was a thousand feet from the singing birds to the nearest electrical outlet and we had only fifty feet of rubber-covered extension cord.

Jerry bought eighty feet more, then a 250-foot reel at

Sears; I went shopping, came home with 900 feet of intercom wire discarded at a junk yard by a seismograph crew. The wire cost $9.00—a bargain! We spent two long days scraping, matching, and joining the eight pairs of wires into two pairs, splicing the breaks, and building reels. We now had nearly 2000 feet of good (?) power wire. The insulation was rather thin on the bargain wire and, at later inconvenient times, we had to locate shorts and discard sections.

The first time we used one of the homemade reels it collapsed like a wet fish net. Jerry then reinforced all the reels so thoroughly that we often wished for a husky boy to help lift them. As recording methods and conditions gradually changed, the power reels were supplemented with several reels of microphone wire.

The thrushes at Gilliam's waited several days for us, but in four predawn trips we failed to get a microphone close enough to a singing bird to produce a satisfactory recording. It is hard to predict just where a migrating bird's song perch will be.

One day a mockingbird sang for an hour from the swamp holly tree in our backyard and much of his song got on our tape. Jerry wondered how it would sound as background music for a recital of Whitman's poem about a mockingbird song, *Out of the Cradle Endlessly Rocking.* The first step was an immediate-playback phonograph copy of the bird song, made on our portable phonograph-recorder.

Dorothy England, good friend and fellow birder, finally agreed to give the recitation. She came over to our house, Jerry set the tape in motion and Dorothy began. He had enjoyed the poem for many years but never before had he heard Dorothy in recital—and I had neglected to tell him she is a graduate of the Emerson School of Expression. He was so spellbound he almost forgot to manipulate the controls of the two machines.

5

A disc copy of this prized combination of poem embellished with mocker was sent to Roy Bedicheck, the famous author-naturalist who helped to immortalize the mockingbird in his first book, *Adventures of a Texas Naturalist*.

"Please congratulate, for me, the lady who recites the poem," he wrote to us. "She does a wonderful job of weaving the words and rhythm into the song itself."

Out in the northwest part of the county we hoped to get away from traffic racket. A month earlier we'd heard both white-throated and white-crowned sparrows singing contentedly along a brushy ravine where it was crossed by a narrow, country lane. The winter sparrows were still there and singing. Nearby we also heard lark sparrows, dickcissels, and a blue grosbeak. But the nearest farmhouse where we might have secured electric power was a full half mile away. Those winter sparrows were unattainable.

In the beautiful Woodland Springs Camp, south of Dallas, we set up our equipment before daylight one morning. The tape ran for twenty minutes while a tufted titmouse, a friendly little bird whose beady eye and saucy crest belie his Quaker dress, went through all his repertoire, the best variety we ever heard from the species. Titmouse songs rarely have more than one or two notes, repetitious but musical. At home we discovered that not one note had been recorded! It was finally agreed that one of us had forgotten to plug in the microphone —also agreed not to try to decide which one.

One day at Lemmon Lake, south of Dallas, we found a cardinal which was singing a song we had not heard before. The new song was promptly recorded. A week later we recorded almost the same peculiar song from another cardinal about ten miles west of the first bird. It was a descending cascade of staccato notes and seemed to be a special regional song.

About two years later came testimony as to another regional

song, while we were giving a recital for the Camp Fire Guardians of Dallas.

"Oh, that's a *Kentucky* cardinal!" one of them interrupted. "I have been listening in vain for that particular song ever since we moved to Texas." She was right; the song had been recorded near Louisville.

On the other hand, some cardinal patterns, or tunes, in addition to the simpler ones of a few repeated notes, seem to be widespread. My mother used to interpret one of these, in Kansas, as "Where is Hugh, Hugh, Hugh, Hugh, Hugh?" This, or the similar "what to cheer," we heard later in Florida, Kentucky, Texas, Louisiana, and states between.

Realization was growing that, among certain species of birds, variations of songs are almost endless. One of our special objectives became the recording of as many different melodies as we could find from each individual bird as well as from the species. Trying for a variety of species was taken for granted.

One stimulant to our recording efforts was the fact that such southerly favorites as the titmouse, painted bunting and Carolina chickadee, the species in Texas, were not on the well-known early Cornell University records. When giving bird programs illustrated with colored slides and the records, it had been fairly easy to whistle imitations of the titmouse. But our southern chickadee sings far too high and the painted bunting too fast for an amateur bird imitator.

It was a red-letter recording day when we taped the calls and wood chopper-like hammering of a pileated woodpecker, and right in metropolitan Dallas County. How his red crest glowed above the black body! Beginners' luck! We had always considered it a special day even to *see* a pileated woodpecker. Later, we were ready to agree with other observers that these crow-sized birds are neither as shy nor as rare as they were twenty-five, even ten years ago.

7

After an article about our new hobby appeared in the Dallas *Times Herald,* a woman living in our own neighborhood called to tell us that a painted bunting was singing regularly from a utility pole in her alley. She offered to donate "a cupful of mike juice" via her back-porch light socket. Because she could tell us so exactly where to hoist our microphone, by next sunrise we had a good recording of the rapid warble of a painted bunting. It was another of our lucky days.

How often we wished, as we were playing Boswell to the birds, that we had wings to follow them! No swamp, no mountaintop, no trackless forest, tangled thicket, or prickly desert could thwart us. We could really get away from traffic noises. (We forgot that most birds seem to prefer to be somewhere near human habitation.) Then all we'd have left to worry about would be wind and water noises, finding the birds we wanted, and persuading them to sing for us. If not wings then a magic carpet please, Ali Baba, to carry us and our recording equipment! We could use about 1000 pounds if we didn't have to carry it. And cloaks of invisibility would come in handy. While we were dreaming we equipped the cloaks with automatic heaters, for birds sing best and breezes are least around the ever amazingly chilly hours of dawn and sunrise.

We were learning by experience that it takes plenty of time and patience to get good recordings of wild bird songs. In later years Jerry often introduced our informal recitals with:

"Birds do not sing at the nod of a conductor, or in a soundproof room. A microphone which amplifies a bird song also turns a breeze into a tornado and attracts the sound of trucks the way a magnet draws tacks. Our dealings are with characters more temperamental than any prima donna who ever graced the Metropolitan."

Poetical friends who think breezes and brooks musical just haven't tried to record them. And a chorus of bird songs coming to the ears from all directions is something else which is better enjoyed on the spot, not secondhand.

On May 29 we played our new recordings for a small group of nature-minded friends. Our recital included more or less satisfactory recordings of these bird voices: cardinal, summer tanager, mockingbird, Carolina wren, tufted titmouse, bluejay, red-eyed vireo, white-eyed vireo, Bell's vireo, red-winged blackbird, mourning dove, crow, crested flycatcher, yellow-billed cuckoo, red-bellied and pileated woodpeckers, and indigo and painted buntings. Here were eighteen species in our first two months of recording. But many of them were marred by unwanted noises.

By the first of June the best of the recording season is over, in a region as far south as Dallas. The only additional bird voices we taped that first summer, well enough to be worth saving, were an orchard oriole, whose rich coat of chestnut and black assured us that his wiry warble was from a mature male, and a blue grosbeak. Both of these colorful birds seemed to prefer the lacy shade of mesquite pastures, typical of the western half of the county.

Our recording gear having outgrown the capacity of our sedan, in June we traded it in on a new, half-ton, panel truck. Inside, Jerry built three shelves along each side, each shelf enclosed by three little doors, eighteen doors in all, each with a latch and two hinges. Each of his tools, including two saws, three hammers, six screwdrivers, a carpenter's brace, and a small electric drill, had its own special holder.

On July 3, our spring fever reached a peak. We suddenly decided to sell our home, buy a house trailer, and follow the bluebirds.

"We can't record bird songs around Dallas, too many trucks and planes," Jerry explained to friends who were shocked to learn we were planning to leave the cottage we had tucked between giant oaks, our wildflower garden so filled with birds,

9

our precious books. I just smiled and tried to concentrate on my losing struggle with dust on the books and Bermuda grass in the flower beds.

"Good for you! You are going to do what we always dreamed of, take your time and explore all the tempting little sideroads," said other friends. "But who will see that your winter birds are fed?"

"Wish you the best of luck in your new business!" one said, worriedly. We smiled at that idea. We hoped some of the birds might sing for their suppers but expected none to sing for ours. This was just a new game we'd discovered.

The new trailer, delivered on November 12, was a three-room model with all the amenities required by a couple who had outgrown their desire to "rough it." Extra cupboards had been fitted in every nook and cranny. There was space for everything we needed from a portable sewing machine to a typewriter and a slide projector and screen. I even added my six favorite vases and several framed pictures of birds. Jerry installed a block-and-tackle arrangement for lifting one side of the mattress and springs, to improve access to the storage space under the bed. I made about 100 small pads to keep the nuts and bolts from rattling in the truck and the dishes from breaking in the trailer.

We bought air mattresses, dreaming we'd sometimes leave the trailer at the end of a paved road, then, while exploring back country, sleep in the truck. Jerry built a little pushcart, with folding handlebars, for transporting the recording equipment down a wooded trail too narrow for the truck. The air mattresses were never used except for a later family house party. The handcart was used only once, where massive posts blocked the truck. Counting reels of wire and other equipment, Jerry guessed that our truck load weighed more than 1000 pounds.

On December 3, 1948, we were up before dawn. This was

moving day. We wandered around for a farewell look out each window of the cottage, at the stars, then the red dawn flaring behind bare tree branches. We loved our trees in winter too. But we were about to follow the bluebirds.

Soon after the new trailer had been thoughtfully *backed*, by the deliveryman, onto our s-curved driveway, friends began to ask about our itinerary. We didn't have one. Jerry said we'd decide on our destination after we took to the road; that we'd let the dog out and follow him—only we didn't have a dog. Finally he thought up a story:

"I am going to California where I'll pick up pieces of redwood, some spruce in Washington, white pine in Michigan, cedar in Maine, poplar in the Smokies. And I'll whittle h—l out of them in Tallahassee, Florida."

Jerry got experience in backing the outfit that first morning, despite the deliveryman. He pulled out of the driveway into our narrow street, then decided to back up a little. In no time the rear of the trailer was hanging over the walk on one side while the front of the truck nudged the opposite curb.

We spent our first night in a Dallas trailer park, left at five-thirty next morning, heading southeast. The truck was pulling hard; we began to wonder how we could lighten the load. Six vases and three hammers were not mentioned. The trailer kept trying to butt us all the time, except going up hill. We dubbed it "Terrapin Sue."

We covered only eighty miles in our first day of travel. In typical east Texas piney woods we parked in a wide spot beside the road. Using water from our five-gallon can we managed supper and dishwashing. Then we noticed a light ahead, walked a fourth-mile to a country grocery and filling station. The owner said we would be welcome to park in front and hook onto his REA electricity. We were glad to renew the cooling of our refrigerator.

Near Westlake, Louisiana, we found just the kind of trailer

park we were looking for, all modern conveniences even to drainage for our sewer hose; yet it was on a quiet country road, in the woods, and with few other occupants. In a short stroll along a swampy creek back of the camp we saw myrtle warblers, juncos, brown thrashers, chickadees, and a woodcock, the second one we'd ever seen. A yellowthroat sang a few notes.

Big native magnolias, laurel oaks, live oaks, and sweet gums shaded the trailer park. Spanish moss did not seem to thrive on the living pine trees; others were heavily shrouded with the gray drapery. Swamps were filled with scrub palmettos. Turtles were everywhere. Ships berthed in a canal of the region appeared to be floating in a prairie of saw grass. Roadside ditches were filled with thick, floating leaves of water hyacinths, a few of their lavender flower clusters still present. Floating evening primroses, which have little, four-petaled yellow flowers, were still in bloom. Yaupon berries looked like red currants. Yaupons are not as showy as their relative, the deciduous "swamp" holly, because their fruits are partly hidden by the dark, small, scalloped, evergreen leaves.

Oil willows lighted up a few dark, swampy spots, the fluffy, feathered seeds giving, from a distance, the effect of white flowers. Juba's bush, not a bush but a weed found in low woods, also bursts into a feathery white cloud as it goes to seed. Wax myrtle shrubs with olive-green, aromatic leaves and wax-coated seeds, the source of bayberry candles, were also attractive to birds.

We became aware of a constant roar; it came from a butyl-rubber plant a mile away, and it ran night and day! Oh well, December is a poor month for bird songs anyway. Westlake was lovely but recording bird songs would never be possible there.

On December 13, we hitched up Terrapin Sue and set out for Florida. All went well until we reached a stretch of pavement slick from a recent overflow of muddy water. Terrapin Sue began to buck and shy. We slowed to thirty miles an hour but it was too late. She had the bit in her teeth.

"This is it," said Jerry calmly as she gave us a final push toward a swampy ditch.

"Jerry!" I quavered as I came to, lying in the truck roof, "I'm alive. Are you?"

"Alive, too, and I smell gasoline!" Jerry answered, "Let's get out of here!"

We surveyed a sorry mess—our rainbow cruise bogged down in a Louisiana mudhole! I felt like crying until I looked at Jerry, sitting against a telephone pole, a humped-up lump of dejection.

The truck, upside down and reversed end for end, was crushed on the top and one side. Terrapin Sue, right side up, was still in good shape. That is she was, until the "wreckers," trying to pull her back on the road, tore a long gash in her side and broke a window.

We left the truck in Louisiana to be repaired and summoned a driver to take us and the trailer back to the trailer factory in Fort Worth. The bird recorders had to back up to make a new start.

The Travelite factory owners were very kind to us, and let us continue to live in our trailer while repairs were being made. True, we were out of one mudhole into another, but we felt more comfortable as neighbors to the freight engines, which banged and hissed and tooted all night, than with the pitiful, hopeless folks in the Louisiana trailer park where we had waited for the driver from Fort Worth.

If we had known in advance that we would be calling the factory yard "home" for sixty-six days, it would have been harder to bear. Fort Worth experienced the coldest winter in years. Rains froze on tree branches and power wires until many were broken by the weight. Jerry slipped on the ice, cracked two ribs, bruised his toe, and got a "housemaid's-knee" lump on his elbow which barely escaped an operation.

But friends, new and old, displayed the neighborliness and hospitality for which the "cow town" is famous. A friend from my Camp Fire days drove across town every Saturday to take me shopping for groceries. Another friend took us on birding jaunts. After they had read about us in the Fort Worth *Star Telegram*, the Wallenbergs, bird watchers who lived beside Lake Worth, showed us every kindness. Bob Hardwicke, an oil corporation lawyer whom Jerry had known in the API, gave encouragement to our bird-recording project.

On January 12, 1949, we played our bird songs at a public meeting in the Children's Museum at Fort Worth. One day we played some bird songs at a luncheon of the Pan Am Club, and, at 4 P.M. for the College Club Gardners at the Botanical Center. On February 11 our recital included the Dorothy England mockingbird piece. This program was sponsored by the Fort Worth Council of Garden Clubs. The program chairman introduced us as the "internationally famous Stillwells." She was just trying to restore our optimism.

When Jerry was not rebuilding power reels, or tinkering with other odd jobs, he kept busy editing and rearranging the bird tapes. He made phonograph records for a few inquiring friends; their production was one by one and beset by fluorescent light and other interference.

On February 27 our fully repaired trailer was moved to the Samuell Trailer Park in east Dallas. The freight engines and muddy factory yard were replaced by shade trees and grassy lawn. We got back to Big D just in time to help plan a luncheon promoting the new Audubon Nature Camp at Kerrville, Texas. At the trailer park we managed to record a cardinal, a titmouse, and a Carolina wren. Primrose Jamieson, my sister-in-law, was our transportation angel for the grocery shopping. The "Looseana boys" *still* did not have our truck repaired.

14

We began to hunt around for friends with influence; the repairman had not been able to get the new parts from the Ford factory. On March 28 we at last got word that our truck was ready for us. If Tay Rall, a friend with influence in the Dallas Ford plant, hadn't moved mountains, no telling how much longer we would have been held up.

As we were bringing the truck back through Louisiana we noticed large clumps of pale pink blossoms among the pines. At first we thought they were dogwood but closer looks showed they were wild azaleas; they bloom on shrubs and the branches do not have the layered effect so typical of dogwood. From Marshall, Texas, westward for several miles, we found wisterias in bloom, some along the fences, others climbing high into the pines. They made one of the most attractive roadside plantings we had ever seen.

After further minor revisions to both truck and trailer we were ready to resume our travels. Since April seemed a little early to start north we decided to accept the invitation of the Gills' (bird enthusiast friends of ours) to park at their place in "The Valley," as the lower Rio Grande region is called by Texans. Their home, two or three miles west of Harlingen and a mile off the main highway, should be a good place for bird recording.

Chapter II

"THE VALLEY"

Now is the winter of our discontent made glorious summer. . . ." What a contrast to the mud and din we had been living with all winter! Terrapin Sue, our recalcitrant trailer, was parked in the Gills' driveway, between their citrus grove and pansy-bordered garden.

"The Valley" is a broad, flat, subtropical region bordered on the southwest by the lower part of the Rio Grande River and Mexico, on the southeast by the Gulf, and northward and westward it merges into the higher desert and dry prairie. Citrus groves and winter vegetable fields have largely replaced not only the native cactus and mesquite, but also, near the river, the hackberry and Rio Grande ash trees as well as more exotic and tropical trees. Many highways are lined with the tall, slender trunks of palms, their leafy heads bending in the breezes. The region is not as famous as Florida winter resorts, but it does attract many winter visitors, known, sub rosa, as "snowbirds."

The Valley is a mecca for ornithologists because of its large population of wild birds, migrants from Mexico, which are rare or unknown in other parts of the country. We suspected that the birds were as influential as the climate in causing the Gills to move from Dallas to Harlingen. Terry and Maurine Gill, gas engineer and businesswoman, hospitably share, with everyone except collectors, their knowledge of where to find

17

the rarer birds. They had several unpleasant experiences with professional collectors, such as having the only individual of a species known to be nesting in the United States shot to extinction right in their own backyard! Terry Gill has taken many beautiful color slides of the Valley birds. His programs are much in demand.

Buff-bellied hummingbirds were partial to the cannas in the Gills' garden. Bird watchers from Connecticut and California, and points everywhere between, came to see these rare birds. We tried and failed to record their squeaks and buzzing wings. Dorothy England, during her visit, spent hours catching them on motion-picture film. Hooded orioles flitted like black and yellow butterflies, nipping holes in the Gills' canna blossoms, whether for nectar or for insects we were not sure. The flittings were only a few feet from our trailer, but the birds wouldn't sing for us. A cute little snub-nosed Sharpe's seedeater did his part; after Jerry had hung a microphone in the Rio Grande ash beside the front door, the bird came back to his favorite perch therein and sang an extended ditty.

Guy Emerson, champion bird lister and retired banker of New York City, helped with the 1949 spring bird census in the Valley. He predicted that it would take us about ten years to get a representative collection of the songs of birds in the United States. We rather expected to run out of both energy and money before then. The two things we did not run out of, in twelve seasons, were enthusiasm and still-unrecorded bird songs. Mr. Emerson was essentially correct.

That winter had been severe on the citrus groves of the Valley. By the time we got down there one third of the citrus trees had been bulldozed and replaced with cotton and vegetables. Terry and a few other orchardists were trying to save some of the trees by pruning out the dead branches. Now fresh leaves were showing here and there on the citrus. Repairs to our truck cupboards were postponed while Jerry kept the wheels of the recorder turning, editing on rainy days.

In addition to the mourning dove, whose contralto cooing is familiar in almost every state in the union, there are five species of doves in the Valley. We gradually learned to recognize their calls as the Gills supplemented the information in Peterson's *Field Guide to Western Birds.* "Western," for both plants and birds, begins at about the 100th meridian. The cardinal-sized Inca dove, with scaly-looking back and rosy pink under the wings, seems to prefer country dooryards. Despite the preoccupations of his human neighbors in a land of citrus groves and orange drinks, the Inca's persistent two-note call is "Cold Coke, cold Coke, cold Coke. . . ." To some people he says "Ball two." Maurine Gill's Mexican maid declares, "Everyone knows the bird is saying *'Sole tu'* [only you]." To dryland farmers he says "No hope."

The smaller Mexican ground dove is much shyer than the Inca and his call much fainter. His soft "Coooo-oo" slurs slightly upward in pitch. According to our records, the similar but stronger call of the eastern ground dove, recorded in Florida, slurs downward.

The white-winged dove, his "Who-cooks-for-you?" unmistakable in its dovelike quality, alternates with "Who-dood-it, who-dood-it, whoo?" He is usually heard only from brushy land. The deep, drawn-out, ghostly "Oo-oo-oo-oo-oo?" of the white-fronted dove seems to come from the far recesses of dense woods. And he is hard to find. The red-billed pigeon, largest of the Valley doves, also prefers low woodlands. His call somewhat resembles that of the whitewing, but includes a more accented note and the triple repetition of four syllables: "Whooooo, who-*took*-a-too, who-*took*-a-too, who-*took*-a-too?" Visits in four more spring seasons and additional equipment were required before we finally secured adequate recordings of all of these doves.

19

A visiting neighbor recited with gusto the antics of some green jays nesting near his home. Two of them had been fighting their own reflections in the polished hubcaps of his automobile. The green jay is a secretive bird, and mischievous, but he has as beautiful plumage as any bird in America. The throat and upper breast are coal black, the crown sky-blue, the back and wings apple green, and the central feathers of the tail are that shade of greenish blue called peacock. The outer tail feathers and the undersides of the wings are canary yellow. One of these birds visited the Gills' dooryard often during the first week or two after we arrived, and we caught *one* of his typical calls on our tape; then he retired to thickets far from reach.

Our trips in search of birds to record took us through the wooded lowlands as well as semidesert country of the Valley. Oleanders, so popular in warm climates in spite of poisonous foliage, were conspicuous among the shrubs and trees used for highway planting. Their bright pink, white, or red flowers stood out against the dark green, dense, glossy leaves. These tall shrubs contrasted well with another much-planted evergreen species, athel or tamarisk, a variety of salt cedar, whose light, silvery-green feathery plumes rose above the compact oleanders. The needlelike leaves of athel resemble the longer, drooping needles of Australian pine, which is not a true pine.

Some of the highways were lined with typical native plants. Many birds found shelter in the huge mounds of prickly-pear cactus, which grew sometimes fifteen feet high and to greater widths. The thick, widely scalloped, leaflike stems were bordered with blossoms, big, yellow, china-silk rosettes. The green-barked Parkinsonia[1] trees, called retama in Texas and paloverde in Arizona, were as fringe-leaved as mesquite, and draped with leis of yellow flowers. They resemble a more

[1] Only the branches of retama are green whereas even the trunk of paloverde remains smooth and green.

20

northerly relative, black locust, with finely divided leaves but blackish bark and long, pronged thorns. Huisache (rhymes with weed-patch) is a favorite among the native acacias for its golden, fuzzy-ball flowers, which are licorice-scented. Blackbrush, a much lower-growing shrub, is much less showy as its fuzzy balls are a pale cream color.

The area around the McAllen Desert pond, some miles west of Harlingen, seemed to be a favorite resort for many birds. The habitat is the semidesert type which extends for many miles north and west from the Rio Grande. The soil is rocky and sandy, the vegetation typical thorny "chaparral," including catclaw, creosote bush, blackbrush, huisache, dwarf ebony, mesquite, and cactus.

Arriving at the pond shortly before daybreak one morning, we heard the curious guttural whinnying calls of a Texas nighthawk, some of the quavering sounds resembling certain calls of a screech owl. The same calls were heard later in the Loma Alta coastal plain, east of Harlingen, where we secured a fairly good recording. The bird rarely flies high in the air and it does not use the "scape" call or the dive-bombing "zoom" of the eastern nighthawk.

At the McAllen site, another day, we recorded three simple variations from one pyrrhuloxia. The bird sang steadily for half an hour while a mocker and a cactus wren discoursed lustily, by turns, in the distance. The high-crested pyrrhuloxia, sometimes called "bullfinch cardinal," has a thick bill and touches of bright red on his plumage. His songs resemble the more simple tunes of a cardinal, although the quality is thinner and he rarely uses the glides often heard from the latter.

Black-throated sparrows were plentiful in the area and we recorded a few of their songs, but always at too great a distance for best quality. Here we also got our first recording of a cactus wren; it is sheer flattery to call his dry, rapid chatter a

21

song. He is almost as large as a thrush and has a streaked breast, more grayish plumage than a wood thrush.

When Jerry went with Terry Gill to this region, on the spring bird census, their attention was attracted by a spirited bit of avian melody which seemed to come from the vicinity of a dead mesquite whose branches rose well above the surrounding vegetation. Keeping behind the clumps of cactus and ebony, the men advanced cautiously until close enough to hear the singing clearly and identify the *two* singers, a mockingbird and a curve-billed thrasher. The eastern brown thrasher usually sings one phrase twice, pausing a fraction of a second before giving another phrase twice, and so on. The curve-billed rarely repeats the same phrase in succession nor does he pause so often between phrases; usually he sings continuously for twenty or thirty seconds, then pauses for five or ten seconds before resuming his warble. In this case they heard none of the pauses. It was as though the entire recital had been rehearsed in advance: the instant the thrasher paused the mocker would take up the song, then stop as the thrasher began again. Only by close watching could they tell which bird was carrying the melody. The duet continued for about fifteen minutes, then the thrasher departed. Instantly the mockingbird became a typical mocker, rising into the air and fluttering back to his perch as he repeated his varied phrases several times.

On the same trip Terry was scouting the highlands while Jerry wandered slowly through a shrubby woodland near a little water hole. Jerry heard a queer sound, close at first but rapidly fading. An oil pipeline ran through the tract and he was reminded of the sound made by a "go-devil," a device which is pushed or forced through pipelines in order to dislodge any obstructions which might retard the flow of oil. But when Terry returned and the sound was described, rather vaguely, as it had been so brief, he immediately said, "That was a blue, or scaled quail, one of the birds we should have on our list."

On our first trip to the Loma Alta coastal plain, near Port Isabel, we drove along a black-top road for twenty-five miles, then two miles on well-graded dirt to a dim trail across the prairie to the mesquite-ebony-cactus of a sparsely wooded tract, at least a mile from any human habitation. Next morning we were up and out by 2 A.M.; before daylight our equipment was ready for a bird, the truck and little auxiliary engine located five hundred feet from the recorder. Scissor-tailed flycatchers began their dawn songs too high in the air, but we ran the recorder anyway. When playing the tape, after returning to the trailer, we heard no scissortails, but we did hear a queer, periodic sound, regular in sequence, sounding rather like snuffling or snoring. Everyone who heard it had a different guess. Machinery? Brahman cattle snoring? An insect perched on the mike? It was not like any of the noises of our own machinery and we knew of no other within hearing distance. Could it be a new "song" from some night bird? Terry suggested it might have been an armadillo, rooting and snuffling. We listened and looked for clues on later visits to the region, but the sounds remain the most mysterious among our little collection of "species unknown."

A light rain fell the day before our third trip to Loma Alta. Usually the wind and sun will dry the road in one day. Again we reached the tract before daylight. There the rain had been heavier; a half mile beyond the graded dirt road, driving across the prairie flat, the headlights showed water in our path. We spent an hour backing and sliding before we got to relatively dry ground. Going home, more rain had fallen on the dirt road and again we slithered. We had thought the north Texas black-waxy mud was slippery, but this was the greasiest clay we had ever seen.

When we reached a two-acre hammock of golden-green

mesquite that muddy morning, Rio Grande meadowlarks were singing in the distance; occasionally a bobwhite called. Botteri's and Cassin's sparrows trilled side by side; one or the other was not where he belonged, according to their reported habitats. In this coastal region a difference of one foot in elevation determines the plant species that grow there. (We tried to relate this to the saying that a rise of 1000 feet in elevation is climatically equal to moving three hundred miles northward.) The Cassin's sweet, plaintive trill is followed by two lower, short notes. The Botteri's song is a rapid jumble of less musical notes. We caught enough of both birds to whet our appetites.

That was the morning we really *caught* a curve-billed thrasher song. We had recorded him at Bluetown Desert, with liberal accompaniment of mockingbirds; near the McAllen Desert pond there had been wind and the sound of our own engine; this morning he sang for thirty minutes in the top of a mesquite tree fifty feet from our recorder, only fifteen feet from the receiver, which hung on a low branch. At times his song was accompanied by willets and nighthawks.

Shortly before the thrasher started we had heard distant dogs; then along came two Mexican sheepherders, two hundred sheep, and three dogs. Every willet and every nighthawk over a mile of grass-covered plain was aroused; they flew back and forth above us, calling and zooming while the thrasher sang. The recorder was on its green-painted box, Jerry in front of it on a folding camp stool. There was a sudden thump and between his feet lay a half-grown jack rabbit, apparently dead. Two of the dogs rounded the edge of the shrubbery island at full gallop; they stopped abruptly when they saw us and fled when I flourished a stick. Jerry held the rabbit until the dogs were gone, for now he could feel a heart thumping. The instant the rabbit was released he vanished into the underbrush.

We reached Hackberry Woods, near Harlingen, one mid-

May morning, at three-thirty. Our routine was well organized: the recorder and the two reels of microphone wire were unloaded deep in the timber; the truck was then driven back 500 feet toward the road, a power line dragged back to the recorder. While I was running out the two mike lines Jerry started the little gasoline-engine generator. Dawn was hinting by the time we had everything ready; we had used an hour stumbling in the dark, blundering into thorny shrubs.

The morning chorus opened with a duet between a Couch's kingbird and a Mexican crested flycatcher, each doing his special dawn song. One of our microphones seemed to be halfway between the two birds. Before their brief recitals were over a Sennett's thrasher took the stage; soon other birds joined in to complete the full symphony. The bird population is often extremely dense in certain parts of the Valley.

A water-filled resaca, one of the outgrown cradles of the Rio Grande, close to the Hackberry Woods, was a special attraction for birds. In fact about all we ever could record there were mixed choruses. This was before we had acquired a parabolic reflector. We had to hang our microphones from branches where we hoped birds would sing. Soon after sunrise the songsters usually had more or less competition from the dusters, single-engined planes used to spread chemicals over the cotton fields.

One morning we thought we heard a small boy trying to whistle, possibly from the Mexican shack across the resaca. He would give about five deliberate notes, as if he drew a separate breath for each note: "Do-re-mi-re-do" followed by a higher, faster, two-note "Who-who?" Some of these got on our tape as we were trying to record a yellow-green vireo, Delta relative of the red-eyed. Listening to the recording that night, Maurine Gill said, "That Audubon oriole must have been rather far away. Did you see it?" So our small boy was an Audubon oriole!

In this woods the Texas sparrows gave their wiry, accelerated notes, all on one high pitch; cardinals, thrashers, wrens, and mockers swelled the chorus. The lower-pitched doves supplied the contralto. One morning a groove-billed ani flapped slowly over our heads, repeating his low, guttural notes. Jerry quickly got the tape in motion—but the playback had no ani. In his excitement Jerry had forgotten to switch to the nearer microphone.

There were chachalacas in the Hackberry tract; "chachalacks" or merely "chacks" to the Valley folks. Both sexes of the species have loud, raucous voices; presumably the lower-pitched "cut-it-out" comes from the male, as "she" answers with a higher, shrewish "keep-it-up," according to the translations of Dr. Allen of Cornell. The dusky birds, like half-grown turkeys, are found in only a few places in this country. The species is on the point of extinction in the United States and certainly decreasing in Mexico as their natural habitats below the border are also being rapidly destroyed.

In 1952 friends wrote us that the Hackberry Woods had been cleared, completely bulldozed! Now only the rustle of corn and cotton is heard where once we heard the orioles, the doves, and the chachalacas.

At last, on May 23, 1949, right in the Gill dooryard and close to our trailer, we secured a good recording of the calls and also the morning or dawn song of the Couch's kingbird. The most typical call is a "whee-er," a downward-slurring note with a faint tremolo, lasting about one-half second, with a pitch drop of about three and one-half tones, the highest note being close to the highest G sharp on the piano. This call is given at random intervals. Another call, used less frequently, has three or four syllables, the first ending with a slight upward slur, the remaining staccato and uniform in pitch. This might be expressed as "Tree-ee, chu-chur" or "Tree-ee, chu-chu, chu-chur." The dawn song consists of two parts, the first

[1] We bought a truck and house trailer in which to "follow the bluebirds." But it was a cardinal we had painted on the truck.

[2] *The giant ebony tree at the semi-tropical Santa Ana Wildlife Refuge near Harlingen, Texas. Voices of chachalacas, kiskadee flycatcher, boat-tailed grackle, and four species of doves are among our souvenirs from that area.*

[3] A snowy egret admires his reflection in this Everglades swamp penetrated by a boardwalk called "Anhinga Trail." Calls of wading birds, from purple gallinules to great blue herons, made a harsh medley of sounds.

[4] *Barges on the Ohio River at Otter Creek, Kentucky, near Louisville. Among our many recordings here were songs of wood thrushes, catbird, orchard oriole, Kentucky warbler and cardinal, towhee and whippoorwill.*

a varying number of repetitions of the whee-er call and the second something like "Treee-eee, treee-eee, tr-whee-er," uttered rapidly in ascending scale but ending with an abrupt downward slur. The song is varied only by the number of times the first part is repeated, sometimes six or eight times, as if he had forgotten the second part and then finally recalled it. The little ditty, taken as a whole, constitutes a definite melody, the most musical we have heard from any member of the flycatcher family.

Our kingbird's singing station was in the top of a hackberry tree; he always chose the same bough and always sang within six or eight inches of the same spot. He sang here for periods varying from five to fifteen minutes, then disappeared for the day. We suspect this dawn recital was given some distance from his nesting territory. A Mexican crested flycatcher whose nest was located fifty feet from the trailer never gave his dawn song close by. We often heard him, or another of his species, about one-fourth mile away.

We spent a lot of time at the Santa Ana Wildlife Refuge in the Valley; it had been established largely as the result of an extended one-man campaign by Irby Davis. Luckily, we were old friends of the Irby Davises. No bird student visits the Valley without seeking to meet him and his biology-teacher wife, the leading ornithologists of the region. Since 1950 he has been spending every spring recording the bird voices of old Mexico. The old, red-tiled roofed mission-style headquarters building was shaded by tall ebony trees whose dark olive-green foliage cast a dense shade in spite of the fact that the leaves are finely divided. A trail-trip to pay our respects to the revered giant ebony, in the heart of the tract, became part of our routine. The refuge is bordered by the Rio Grande and, in years of normal rainfall, has three shallow lakes as well as dense woodlands and sections of semi-desert cactus and mesquite. In addition to ash, elm, and hackberry there were the more tropical anaqua and tepehuaje trees, often interwoven with vines and bushes. When the anaqua, with its rough, leathery leaves, was in bloom its white flower clusters reminded us of apple blossoms. The gray-barked tepehuaje, even when thirty feet tall, resembles a giant fern.

One June morning it was still dark when we stopped by the old building at Santa Ana. One receiver we placed close by, the other 500 feet south in dense woods. Rats were heard scurrying through the deserted house; once a barn owl disappeared inside but it was too dark to see whether he had his rat when he came out. The far microphone was quite sensitive; on two occasions we picked up the braying of a donkey, which must have been in Mexico, one and a half miles away, across the river. A lamp bulb was hung above the recorder placed under the ebonies. Immediately the air around the light was filled with myriads of small insects, less than one-eighth inch long, so numerous the light was dim. Possibly they were Mayflies. In a few minutes the recorder was covered with the insects. The light was moved a dozen feet away. When daylight came the recorder case was found to have a three inch deep layer of insect corpses. Hooded orioles, brilliant in orange and black, flitted through the ebonies, pausing occasionally to give us a few samples of their chattering songs. Two days later, at the same spot, only a dozen of the lacy-winged insects were seen. The orioles were not there either.

When we played back the bird recordings made on that trip to Santa Ana, Irby Davis identified a faint, froglike sound as the voice of the ferruginous pygmy owl; it sounds something like the Mexican tree frog. We got a better recording of the owl a few days later. Its voice is clear and mellow; by partially filling a pint bottle and whuffing his breath across the opening, Jerry produced a note similar in both quality and pitch to that of the little owl.

Many recording trips were made to this refuge during five different years. We learned to negotiate all of the several routes from Harlingen, about twenty-five miles away, without getting lost in the predawn darkness. I can remember most of the birds we recorded there, caught in the lulls between dog barks, donkey brays from across the river, tractors, oil-well pumps, and dusting planes. The voices we thought good enough to be worth saving include: ferruginous pygmy owl (the first evidence of his presence in Texas); barn owl (mostly hisses, but what else can he do?); hooded orioles (weak and helter-skelter songs at best); good and varied chachalaca chatter; two song types from Texas sparrows (both were rapid, wiry accelerations all on one pitch); the lilting melody of a Sennett's thrasher; green jays, with plumage far more beautiful than their voices; a great-tailed grackle[2]; dawn song of a Mexican crested flycatcher; white-fronted dove and red-billed pigeon, both of fair quality, in 1957; a fair screech owl; a cactus wren—a metronome, not a musician; black-crested titmouse in two song types so simple they could hardly be called "patterns"; a golden-fronted woodpecker. Once we caught a Derby flycatcher screaming his "get-ter-heck" at a Harris' hawk twice his size, who was replying only in guttural and probably profane monosyllables. The argument started with a disagreement as to which bird had achieved the more handsome combination of chestnut and black and white plumage. The flycatcher had an advantage by displaying his bright yellow underwear. Cardinals and white-eyed vireos don't count on the Santa Ana list because they gave us no new song patterns.

We were having recording problems. Our crystal microphone was much more sensitive than the dynamic ones. A technician in Brownsville had built for us a little one-tube

[2] This mimicking, posturing clown is on our western record.

amplifier-transformer that enabled us to use the crystal receiver at a distance of 500 feet or more, with very little line loss. But after several weeks this combination had stopped working, seemingly not rugged enough for use in the hot, humid climate of the Rio Grande Valley. Eventually, for field use, the crystals were replaced entirely by dynamic microphones.

To add to our problems, the gas-engine generator was misbehaving. It had been recommended by a Dallas expert, was one-half horsepower, guaranteed to give 120 volts AC, 300 watts, and sixty cycles. Jerry had mounted the unit on heavy redwood, inside a framework of welded pipe. The factory muffler had been replaced at once by a Ford muffler. There was still too much noise, even when we parked the truck and engine 500 feet from the recorder; too many of our bird songs were marred by the racket of the exhaust. Despite claims regarding the regulator, the speed went wild. Finally Jerry managed to adjust the governor for the load of 150 watts required by our recorder. The gasoline had to be white, not ethyl; the tank held two quarts and had to be refilled about every half hour.

There was also a residual hum in many of our recordings. Terry Gill finally got most of it out with a stock filter, a good ground, and orientation of all wires.

We had adopted the slogan "Follow the Bluebirds!" It sounded fine and we wanted a bluebird painted on the truck. But the truck was green. I found a sign painter who agreed to paint a cardinal for us. As a model we gave him a portrait of the bird by Don Eckleberry, who had painted the bird portraits for Pough's *Audubon Bird Guides*. But our cardinal was queer; his legs were joined to his body about like a pied-billed grebe's. We hoped to find someone to do the job over but never did. It brought various reactions. Some observers assumed we had some connection with, or interest in, the Saint Louis Cardinals; a grocery store helper thought we were rivals from the Cardinal Food Stores. One day a man came up to our parked outfit with:

"Say! What's your pitch? I used to be in show business myself."

Our desire to erase the cardinal grew as we belatedly realized that Cornell was using a cardinal likeness in advertising its records.

On June 25 we reluctantly broke away from the Gills and their charming dooryard and the fascinating birds of the Valley. The recorder was acting up and Jerry had decided a visit to the factory was in order. We both wanted to try for birds in a different part of the country. We started on our travels again, heading north. I had my heart set on recording a hermit thrush.

Chapter III

FEW BIRDS, BUT FRIENDLY FOLKS

THE first stop on our northward trip was at Kerrville, Texas. While in this "hill country" of the central part of the state, we took a thirty-mile jaunt up the cypress-lined Guadaloupe River, hoping to record a canyon wren. Several were heard, blending their rapturous, cascading melodies with the sounds of the limpid, rippling stream. But alas, the stream was always much closer and louder than the bird!

Business matters at Dallas included a heavier driving motor installed in the tape recorder; it seemed to help for a while. After hurried visits with friends we pulled north again at four o'clock one morning. That day we drove nearly three hundred miles, but decided it was too far for one day when dragging a trailer. It was one of the few days when we had to buy ice to keep our refrigerator cool. Progress was more leisurely through the Ozark hills of southern Missouri.

We turned off US 60 a few miles from the Big Spring State Park in southeast Missouri. As we were hesitating beside the road, a man in a pickup truck stopped to ask if we were in trouble. To our inquiry about the side road into the park he advised that it was rather steep and narrow in places. He suggested we leave our trailer in front of his house, nearby, where he would be glad to supply us with electricity and water. Thus we met Mr. and Mrs. Paul of Van Buren. One day Mrs. Paul came out to our trailer with a delicious boiled dinner, saying cooking was her hobby. Could it be that we were growing old enough to receive the solicitude old folks and babies often inspire?

The Pauls were the first among many roadside acquaintances, in addition to old friends, and friends of friends, and others interested in birds, who went out of their way to show us various kindnesses, unexpected little expressions of hospitality. If the Sam Walter Foss verse has become trite, it is because it expresses such a prevalent impulse:

Let me live in a house by the side of the road
And be a friend to man.

The Big Spring was beautiful. Nearby we taped a summer tanager song, without the "Genevieve" phrases of our Dallas bird.

Southeast of Chicago we got mixed up in a traffic jam. Perhaps you have found yourself past the intersection of two six-lane, big-city highways at 5 P.M., headed toward the business center you wanted to avoid. But have you ever tried to make a U turn under such conditions, with a house trailer dangling behind you? It required magic as well as good luck. The good luck was in finding a right turn into the trucking yard of a wholesale warehouse. The magic was in the white glove of a local traffic dispatcher who sympathized with our predicament and cleared the way for our left turn.

Our overnight stop at Bloomington, Illinois, was in a trailer park with a grassy lawn and big silver maple trees. At break of dawn we caught the cheerful, tuneless carol of a robin, our first recording of the species. His is usually the first song heard in the morning.

On July 8 we reached Michigan, where we paused for information at a state highway station. The Stillwells are early birds; we waited for an hour until a young woman arrived, invited us in, and offered to help. Mrs. Dorothy Anderson was so helpful we felt impelled to write to the head office of the highway department about her. Quite possibly she did not know the difference between a hermit thrush and a song sparrow, but she was understanding when we outlined our interests and our camping needs, preferably well away from the highway.

"You must visit the Warren Woods," said she. She was indefinite as to the route, advised us to go to Lakeside and inquire there. "Now about a spot to park your trailer. . . ." She stayed on the telephone for more than an hour while we rested, watching the robins on the lawn and under the trees in the parking area beside one of Michigan's busiest highways.

Finally Mrs. Anderson came with the answer and we'll never know what wires were pulled. Down the road, turn left at the Y.W.C.A. sign, ask for the caretaker, and he would show us the garage area. There was about an acre of level ground with open sheds for car storage along one side; the ridge which overlooked Lake Michigan rose steeply on the other side. Between was just fifteen feet more space than the length of our truck and trailer. But we got in, turned around, backed our trailer against the bluff, made a rope suspension bridge for our power line, to keep it out of the way of traffic, and there we were. We trucked down the road for groceries and to mail forwarding cards.

That evening we played some of our bird songs for the Y.W.C.A. campers at their headquarters on the bluff. When we returned to the trailer a whippoorwill was singing close by! The bird sang and our tape revolved during the fifteen-minute intervals between the trains on the New York Central's double tracks. Outside neon lights bothered us. But our tape, on playback, was completely silent. We wondered what had gone wrong.

The next morning we went back to Michigan City, which is in Indiana. Bob Schillinger, the chief engineer of radio sta-

35

tion WIMS, was out at the transmitter. We found his tape recorder, played our tape, but still heard nothing. He came back and tinkered with our machine for two hours. Suddenly it came to life. He didn't know what happened and we never found out.

"Certainly not! Only too glad to help, if I did help." He refused to accept even a case of beer, Jerry's idea of orchids for engineers.

One morning, scouting, we found the Warren Woods. Many times we roamed through this tract which had never known a woodsman's ax. American elms, four feet or more in diameter, were the largest we had ever seen, with one exception. *Our* biggest elm grew in the Canville Creek bottom in southeastern Kansas. It towered above its fellows, a landmark visible for miles, when Jerry and his father walked through those woods over a half century ago. A local butcher's need of a new chopping block caused the monarch's fall.

We liked to brag about the big trees we had seen, but sooner or later we always met someone who had seen a bigger one of the species mentioned. A man told of an elm tree he had seen in 1919 near Marietta, Ohio, a tree thirty-two feet in circumference, with a branch spread of 165 feet, so the man said. In northeastern Ohio in 1924 we had seen a staghorn sumac with a diameter of ten inches; but the elm-man had seen one ever-so-much bigger. Now, at Lakeside, Michigan, we saw a sassafras trunk eighteen inches in diameter, and on the nearby estate of Harold H. Swift we saw our largest black locust.

Mr. Cook, the superintendent of grounds for the Harold Swifts, was a bird observer; he told of a Christmas census when wintering towhees were found in Warren Woods, when those birds should have been far south. Apparently they had lingered because of abundant food protected here by a heavy mantle of fallen leaves. Now, at a swale in Warren Woods a water thrush teetered all around the pool of water but would not sing for us. Mr. Cook thought that the water thrush near his house might still be singing early in the morning. We were in the grounds and ready to record before daylight; the water thrush was there but refused to sing.

Nearly eleven years later came this letter, forwarded to me in Dallas.

HAROLD H. SWIFT
LAKESIDE, BERRIEN COUNTY
MICHIGAN

Clarence D. Cook   *February 13, 1960*
Superintendent of Grounds

Mr. Jerry E. Stillwell
Route 2, Fayetteville, Ark.

Dear Mr. Stillwell:

If you are still at the above address and this letter reaches you I shall be very pleased.

In the midst of our Christmas mail in 1952 I received a Christmas card from you with a message on the back asking for some information. When the Christmas "haze" cleared up and I was catching up on my correspondence I was unable to locate your letter. Just last week when Mrs. Cook was looking over some boxes of old Christmas cards she ran across yours . . . and now, a little over seven years later, is your reply.

The tree next to our residence about which you inquire is a black locust. Here are the dimensions:

circumference 2 ft. above the ground 169½ inches
        "   3   *"*   173½ *"*
        "   4   *"*   180   *"*
        "   4½ *"*   183½ *"*

The circumference was influenced strongly by the fact that the tree was allowed to branch out very low. I do not believe it was a multiple trunk. The circumference of Michigan's largest black

37

locust on the list made up by the Michigan Botanical Society in 1956 was 173 inches.

Very truly yours,
CLARENCE D. COOK

One day we stopped at the first house west of Warren Woods. Boxes of red raspberries were lined up for sale on the front porch. Mrs. Peters, a widow, was living there alone. Her eighty acres extended along one side of the woods; a wood thrush sang behind her house; and a song sparrow; and a house wren. The berry sale completed, she said to our request:

"Why yes, I guess so, though that's pretty early. What about the electricity?" Jerry loosened the bulb in her back-porch light, suggested she leave the indoor switch turned on. She agreed.

We were back early and recorded some of Mrs. Peters's birds. Then Jerry exercised some of his salesmanship. I talked too.

"Why yes, I guess so," she finally agreed, "though I don't see how you're going to get your trailer into that little drive-way. And I haven't enough garden hose to reach that far." We had the hose.

All hobbyists claim, for their own hobby, whether they collect stamps or knit rugs, that they make friends with "such interesting people," meaning those with a hobby similar to their own. But we also liked to remember friendly folks who were not even interested in birds. "Texas Couple Carries on at Famed Warren Woods" read a headline in the St. Joseph, Michigan, paper. The story, plotted by our landlady, removed any suspicions about the nature of our carryings-on and even bestowed an unearned doctor's degree on Jerry. Warren Woods was a beautiful sanctuary of huge native trees, elms, oaks, ash. Yet we will remember the place longest for our hospitable landlady at the edge of the forest, who taught us to add red currants to our red raspberry preserves to make them jell better. Both fruits came from her bushes and we had enough to send two dozen half-pints to Dallas friends.

The Great Lakes region is famous for its fruits and, we always thought, for their especially delicious flavors. We arrived late for most bird songs but found consolation in a variety of cherries from pale and sweet to dark and sour and fresh-pitted, in apples, raspberries, red currants, strawberries—everything to stimulate my most domestic trait, a fondness for making jelly and preserves. The grocers in the towns usually offered only oranges, bananas, and California Bing cherries—imported fruits. But every farmyard had a fruit stand. I can still shut my eyes and see the tiered rows of homemade jelly glowing like jewels as the sun shone through them.

Bordering Warren Woods and a hundred yards back of our trailer was a tangled mass of second-growth woodland where lived a towhee and an indigo bunting. One attraction was the wild blackberries, larger than any we had ever seen in the Ozarks. Every morning a microphone was placed at some spot in the thicket, then shifted the next morning to a location several yards away. But it took many days before we could guess correctly as to which singing perch would be used on which morning. The towhee's "drink tea" differed slightly from any towhee song we ever heard elsewhere.

We had better luck with the wood thrush. He sang all day long, although his interest seemed to wane as the day progressed. At 6 A.M. he sang about every six seconds; at 8 the intervals between songs had increased to about eight seconds; at 10 he sang at twelve-second intervals; about fourteen seconds at noon and by 3 P.M. he was pausing about sixteen or eighteen seconds between songs.

The recorder was causing us trouble. We told Mrs. Peters we were leaving the trailer but would be gone with the truck for two or three days. After trips to repair shops in Toledo and Michigan City and telephone calls to the converter fac-

39

tory in Detroit, we finally acquired a six-volt converter which Jerry spent a day mounting and housing.

We like to remember Mrs. Peters. The day before we left her place she inquired casually how we managed to keep things in our refrigerator, traveling around as we did. Early next morning, after we were hooked up to go, she came to the trailer with a dressed fryer. What a woman! We have thought of her many times.

While we were driving along a country road near Cadillac, Michigan, Jerry spied a martin house and an elderly man working in his garden. Jerry got out, walked to the fence, and growled:

"How in the world do you expect to get martins to live in that house under the trees? Get it out in the open!"

"So *that's* what's wrong!" The man's expression changed slowly; then he smiled. "We wondered . . ."

Other birds were vocal thereabout. The two Leonard men, father and son, invited us to return. They were milking, electric lights showing from the barn when we drove in next morning with the recorder. A song sparrow began telling the world all about it, first with one song, then with another. We caught three different tunes from him. Barn swallows chattered excitedly from the barn roof—until we hoisted a microphone. A chipping sparrow sang here and there, everywhere except near our receiver. An hour later, as we were packing up, Mrs. Leonard invited us into her spotless kitchen-breakfast room, served fresh, lucious red raspberries sweetened with honey and covered with yellow jersey cream—a dish fit for royalty! The chipping sparrows nibbled at coarse meal and chicken-scratch on the kitchen porch, three feet from where we were feasting.

I asked about hermit thrushes. Son Lawrence said they had sung a month ago—"Now wait, was it a hermit or a wood thrush?"—he wasn't sure. The family came to our trailer one evening, bringing big, red strawberries. We played our Warren

Woods wood thrush: yes, that was their bird. So we knew we had to keep on looking.

On the other side of the lake, a grouse ran across the road in front of us; a man said the loons had stopped calling a month ago. In the Cadillac office of the federal forest service a biologist said a hermit thrush might be still singing in the Peninsula but that we would find no accommodations in the forest. Another man in the office finally gave the answer to our repeated questioning. "There is still a little virgin pine in the Hardwicke tract." He gave us directions for finding it. We left the trailer in Cadillac and drove north in the truck.

In the Hardwicke State Park we reached an open space with log buildings; then we walked, and there was the white pine! Forty acres of primeval trees which the man Hardwicke had refused to sell to the lumber barons. Jerry gasped, sat down to stare upward. Big trees always left him a little breathless. The largest specimen was thirteen feet in circumference and 150 feet tall. Someone has called the white pine the most aristocratic of all trees; Julia Rogers called it majestic; we like it best of all pines, especially for the fineness of its needles, forming soft, blue-green plumes. We were grateful that Mr. Hardwicke had refused to sell his trees. Two ruffed grouse slipped away through the underbrush. It was midday and we saw few birds.

Driving farther through the park we reached the spot assigned to trailers: electricity, cooking water carried from the single hydrant, the usual "telephone booth" standing back in the brush. Our brief and negative survey of the prospects was almost completed when the welcoming committee advanced—the owner of the only trailer in sight. He talked so fluently that he left us guessing as to his previous vocation; possibly hawker with a traveling medicine show. He told us with gusto how, of late years, he collected "rabbis" in old Mexico and he proudly exhibited one of his treasures, a curiously formed vegetable product which we thought, at first glance, might have been a fossil; but our questions brought only vague and elusive replies. Maybe he feared we might try to horn in on his pitch. We still wonder what the thing was which he called a "rabbi."

As we drove north from Traverse for twenty-five miles or more, Lake Michigan was sparkling blue on both sides of our road. A tattered banner, stretched across the road, proclaimed: "The Cherry Center of the World." But the orchards had been stripped of their crops. Near Paw Paw, at a roadside stand, we had found the last of the big, dark red Montmorencys, sour but the best-flavored of all cherries.

It seemed we had reached northern Michigan too late for our hermit thrush; we'd have to try again the next spring. Heading south, birds were plentiful, but so were the roars of traffic. Wild, scarlet chokecherries were ripe and beautiful, but we had missed our only chance for the rare Kirtland's, or jackpine, warbler. We had known we were getting a late start on this northward trek, a mistake we never repeated. Better too early than too late, in both hour and season, for recording bird songs.

August 9 did seem early to be heading south, but Jerry was haunted by the previous, extremely cold winter in Fort Worth. And we'd amble, not gallop. The going was easy, slopes gentle and traffic light, a big, shady roadside park at lunchtime, and the larger towns were bypassed.

Ohio was much as we remembered it from residence in 1924 and 1925: massive, well-built red barns, sleek dairy herds, occasionally a bearded Mennonite and his bonneted lady moving leisurely along the road shoulder in a horse-drawn buggy. It wasn't the seventy-five-mile detour or the twenty-five elapsed years that kept us from revisiting Conneaut and Ashtabula. It was Jerry's nightmarish memories of those two winters when he had worn out ten sets of tire chains keeping mainline gas meters open in subzero weather.

On our previous visit to Cleveland, in the truck, we had been fouled in traffic; this time we kept well to the south. At 3 P.M. we asked a filling station man where we could find a parking spot for the night and he said, "Right here." He had a big, concreted parking lot, but we must not stay longer than one week, "city regulations," although this was outside the city limits of Cleveland.

After a telephone call, the Richard Kleins, birding and photographing friends of the Gills, and the Don Eckleberrys (he the bird artist, she a successful designer) came over to see us. What a talk fest! They promised one of them would come over the next day and take us exploring for a better trailer site.

After 150 miles of exploring we were taken to look at the home place of W. G. Scheele, director of the Cleveland Museum of Natural History. He lived thirty miles south of the city, in the Kirtland Hills Reserve. The place suited us just fine and the owner was willing. Soon we were parked in his big back yard, well away from traffic and with a wooded creek nearby.

Sundays, Dick Klein took us birding; weekdays we'd drive into the city to the recorder factory, or a truck repair shop, or a tire store. Three times we got lost, once because a left turn was prohibited, then because a street sign was behind a billboard, and the third time because of plain, everyday dumbheadedness on our part. Country-town beginnings are hard to outgrow.

One Sunday Dick Klein showed us a church belfry in a village square, where barn owls lived. Then he took us to a real bog. We recalled a fifth-grade reader horror story about some children who were lost in a bog. And here we were, products of a prairie state, venturing into the famous Pymatuning bog!

43

The trees were tall and intertwining branches caused a gloomy twilight. Klein kept a fence line always in sight, told us to step only on the tree roots. Silence reigned among the deep shadows. I felt I had a minor adventure when my foot slipped and sank knee-deep in the thick, black mire; it would have sucked off any footgear looser than my high, laced boots. I called for help, although I insisted I could have pulled myself out of it—but not without getting covered from both feet to shoulders with the muck.

Later, Dick showed us the really tricky footing along the marshy border of a small lake where we walked on a floating mat of roots which sank just enough to get the soles of our shoes wet. We clung to branches of surrounding bushes, were reminded to avoid the poison sumac so common in such swampy places. If a foot had broken through the root matting, that foot, at least, would have been in the pond. Two daring adventures in one day, both because we had "Daring Dick" to lead us!

There were other side trips around Cleveland. Standing at the border of the big bog, Dick imitated the barred owl and got an answer from far down in the swamp. One evening, standing in the Kleins' yard, Don Eckleberry got answers from two barred owls; that was in Chagrin Falls, a residential suburb of Cleveland. Our friends took us up and down some little-used roads in flatlands where we saw some Henslow's sparrows; a lake where people gathered on the dock to watch the carp, the water boiling when the big fellows, ten and fifteen pounds each, fairly crowded each other out of the water to get the stale bread scraps being tossed to them. And coots walked, flapping, on the backs of the squirming fish to join the feast. Vera Carruthers, secretary of the Kirtland Bird Club, took us to a wonderful tract—big trees, lots of white oaks, a rocky cliff and a valley with clear, purling water. It was August—everyone knows birds won't sing in August.

44

One evening we were due at the Kleins; the most faithful of the Kirtland Bird Club were coming there to hear some of our recordings. The day was a memorable one. In the afternoon Jerry reviewed the reels we would use and found that Dorothy England's recital of the Whitman poem was in bad order because of sticky splices on the tape; this was the first but far from the last time we had trouble with sticky splices. They were dusted with talcum powder.

It was twenty miles or more from our trailer to Dick's place in Chagrin Falls, where we were invited, and Jerry insisted on starting early—we might get lost or have a flat tire. Are all husbands like that? Will they never learn that a hostess doesn't want the guests to appear until the roast duck is about ready to serve? Well then, what time did she say? Neither of us could remember; we compromised on five-thirty. Isabel Klein rose to the occasion:

"Make yourselves at home; Dick's books are mostly over there; he just telephoned he'd be late getting in, detained at Warren."

Then a tasty meal, just for us, the small son, and our hostess. I finally wormed it out: we had NOT been expected for dinner! What would you have said? A gallant hostess helped us to forget our embarrassment. The evening guests seemed to enjoy our bird songs.

On August 22 we were ready for the next lap of our southward journey. As we started to leave our most pleasant site in the kind Scheeles' yard, the trailer got jammed in the driveway between the house and a rock retaining wall beside a deep ravine. We got into many places easily and then had trouble getting out—like a cat with its head caught in a salmon can! A wrecking truck was called, pulled the rear end of the trailer back until we were safe from the ravine. Then we bumped across a field, hurdled a shallow ditch, and reached the highway; the only losses were time and a ten dollar bill.

At first we had tried to avoid routes carrying heavy truck traffic; later we learned that the truck routes were pretty sure to be the shortest and best. Thereafter we followed the trucks on most of our longer hauls. Jerry found a truck driver who knew Pittsburgh, so he said; described in detail the best route for getting through. But somewhere, early, we lost the trail. A mile after crossing the Susquehanna River, we took a wrong turn. The patrolman said we couldn't make a right turn and get back for many blocks and that the hills were too steep for our outfit. Jerry said, "You look the other way when I get to that next corner." The Pittsburgh policeman was a true gentleman—he did look the other way and we made our left turn, two rights, and were on our way again. He waved genially as we sailed by.

On the east side of town we found another trailer camp about two miles from the turnpike entrance; during rush hours four lanes of vehicles, bumper to bumper, passed our parking site.

Leaving the Pennsylvania Turnpike at Carlisle, we lingered a few days to let our mail catch up with us. All of our recording trips were made with very flexible schedules, both as to time and routes. There was no way to foretell just when or where we would find recordable bird songs. But we kept family and friends well posted as to where we had been. Jerry's cryptic postcards often brought smiles—to those who could read his handwriting.

"If a wood duck would just talk, we would make his words immortal. Yours, Jerry Stillwell." Or, "We can't tell a song sparrow where to sing, but yesterday we engineered an engine away from the bird." Or, "We're just living from can to mouth and breathing only between bird songs."

In southeastern Pennsylvania and adjacent Maryland many of the villages had narrow streets, no front lawns or porches. The houses, usually of red brick and with white window shutters, were survivors of colonial days. We natives of the wide open spaces often wondered why houses in the East, even in villages, were built so close to each other. Was it just a habit brought over from England and Europe, where living space really is limited? Reasons for some exceptions were obvious: huge granite boulders, sometimes house-size, were transformed from obstacles into garden landscape assets.

It was not the houses built against the sidewalks but the narrow streets that bothered us. Filling our gas tank often was a problem, not only in colonial villages but elsewhere. The station must be on our side of the road; few pumps had hose long enough to reach the far side of our truck. There must be sufficient space to get the rear end of the trailer off the highway and then room to return to the highway without danger of swinging the rear end into a pump. At first Jerry carried two one-gallon cans of gasoline in a truck cupboard; they survived the Louisiana incident but were discarded forthwith.

At one station we stopped and filled the gas tank. I dashed across the street for a loaf of bread, delayed only shortly by traffic. The station man brought Jerry his change. In one minute he was back, muttering about blocking his driveway, although no cars were waiting.

Within a mile after crossing the Potomac at Point of Rocks in extreme northern Virginia we met Mr. J. C. Nichols. First we saw his trailer park, a two-acre grove of big trees backed by a hill called Furnace Mountain. Across the road, at the back of his well-kept, two-story white house, flowed the Potomac. The park had electricity; water was piped from a spring a short distance up the little mountain. We suggested we'd like to stay a night.

"Well, now, I'd a heap ruther you'd stay a spell," Mr. Nichols said. And we did, ten days or more.

Mr. Nichols was a gentle man, a real Virginia gentleman.

47

He had lived here many years, was now retired. On Sunday afternoons his children brought their children to visit. One Sunday morning Jerry walked over to the house. Nichols sat in front of his radio, his head bowed. He waved Jerry to a chair; the radio prayer went on, then the choir sang.

"I always like to hear that preacher." Nichols snapped off the switch. Jerry forgot his errand, touched by his host's sincere reverence. We soon learned that he practiced his religion on weekdays also. He was an observant man. He knew the trees and the more common birds, some of which he could imitate. We made a little record for his children, giving his whistle-and-talk imitations, but we did not save the original tape. Now I wish we had.

Jerry walked a little on the mountain, thought he saw some ginseng—Klein had pointed out a plant near the Cleveland swamp—and Mr. Nichols was interested, very interested. You may remember ginseng is the plant whose contorted roots still command fantastic prices from Chinese, who consider them as a cure-all drug. The next day the three of us climbed the mountain, walked its length, but Jerry was wrong. Nichols did show us one ginseng plant; the only one, to his knowledge, remaining on the mountain.

Our host wore rubber boots; he finally confessed that he did not care for snakes. We saw a praying mantis six inches long. We looked at the trees; a few chestnuts were staging a comeback after the devastating blight. We also found a chestnut oak. Many years ago Jerry's father had received a few acorns of this species from a friend in Washington—Nichols' Park was only thirty miles from the capitol—and a chestnut oak had grown tall in his Erie, Kansas, dooryard. Some of the trees looked unfamiliar.

"That tree there? Always heard it called 'bomergillyun,'" said Nichols. To be sure, balm-of-Gilead! We found it in our three-volume *Illustrated Flora of the Northeastern States,* by

Britton and Brown. They were among the two-dozen books in our trailer library. We would have been lost without those line drawings.

J. C. Nichols was a big man. One day he came to the trailer carring three tomatoes in one hand; one of them almost filled Jerry's hand. The tomatoes were big and round and red-ripe, the best we ever tasted. Jerry said, "But one of those would make a big meal for us."

"The season's about over," said Nichols. "We've canned all we want and there's more'n we can eat."

The next day he brought over a large basketful of tomatoes, suggesting we could can some. I went to the country store, bought some jars, and canned the tomatoes. Mr. Nichols smiled. "Now when you eat the last of those you'll think of Old Man Nichols up in Virginny!" And think of him we did, a very kindly man. We ate the last of his tomatoes on December 25 in Tampa, Florida. We sent him postcards, now and then, hoping he would remember us.

The night before we left, Mr. Nichols evaded our question, said we hadn't been there long enough to run up his light bill. Early the next morning we pulled to the roadside; no one was up. We slipped a bill under the kitchen door and were on our way.

On either side of the narrow, twisting highway were rock fences built, maybe, a hundred years ago and now smothered under Hall's honeysuckle.

On a side trip from Charlottesville over part of the scenic Skyline Drive, the distant vistas were enchanting, but along that section the highway often ran too far above the trees, not enough intimate glimpses to suit us.

Down the road a day or so Clark's Service Station and Store looked inviting. To our request for trailer space the owner said, "Guess so, if it would be any convenience to you." Jerry added a side-outlet bib to the hydrant, repaired a porch

49

light fixture, and we were happily settled under the shade of two pecan trees. The town of Clarksville, Virginia, was four miles down the road but our host was noncommital about the resemblance of names; he talked about his fox hounds. At every opportunity we visited with Mrs. Clark; we loved her southern accent, but suspected she was inclined to regard us as carpetbaggers.

Later on we were sorry we had not made a collection of human as well as bird voices. It's a wonder we did not follow the example of John Lomax, of folklore fame; he was our next-door neighbor in Dallas. If Browning had asked us, "Did you once see Shelley plain?" we could have answered, "No, but we once saw Carl Sandburg over the back fence," when he visited Lomax. I looked up the Browning poem, remembering only the first line, and not sure of it. The last two verses appealed to me as even more applicable to some of our experiences. From his

Memorabilia

I crossed a moor, with a name of its own
And a certain use in the world no doubt,
Yet a hand's breadth of it shines alone
Mid the blank miles roundabout:

For there I picked up on the heather,
And there I put inside my breast
A moulted feather, an eagle feather!
Well, I forget the rest.

Our eagle feathers were a few special bird songs.

The Clarks' home-cured ham was always on their back-porch table, ready for the knife. I longed to ask her how she cooked it, but was afraid Jerry would accuse me of hinting for a slice.

[5] *Jerry called our first chipping sparrow recording our "thousand-dollar bird song," for it required all the virtues of our new equipment. The Presto recorder, versatile switchbox, and parabolic reflector were acquired during our stay at Otter Creek Park.*

[6] *Many birds, including chats, yellowthroats, and white-throated sparrows were recorded in the thickets and trees at Avian Echoes, near Fayetteville, Arkansas. Wild roses, blackberries, and sumac formed dense tangles.*

[7] *The new, portable Magnemite recorder helped to solve many of our recording problems. It arrived just before we toured the northeastern states for the birds on our second LP record.*

[8] *At Pocono Lake, Pennsylvania, we "caught" our first hermit thrush. On the lake shore I focused first on chattering barn swallows on the utility wire, then faced about and caught a magnolia warbler in a hemlock tree.*

We loafed, cut some records, and roamed the countryside. The main tobacco crop had been harvested although a few Negroes were gathering leaves here and there. There were sketchy glimpses of the Piedmont, where erosion had almost ruined lands that once were flat, now furrowed with deep gullies. Bluebirds and flickers were moving south.

There were still some miles of the Carolinas before we were to see Georgia. After much poring over maps we made the wrong decision: we'd go into South Carolina as far as Columbia and pick up US 1 to Waycross, see the Okefenokee Swamp, then head west.

We saw something of the Carolinas, at thirty miles an hour, holding our course mostly to the western part of the coastal plains, level or only gently rolling. We wanted nothing to do with the Blue Ridge while pulling the trailer. As always, we detoured around the cities whenever possible. Chapel Hill, North Carolina, with its beautiful campus and towering trees looked good for bird life, but we saw no place for house trailers.

The farther we got into Georgia the rougher became US Highway 1. Later we met several travelers who said, "Why, I could have told you to keep off number one; you should have taken number 17!" Georgia—the land of peaches, pecans, and watermelons. And pine barrens. And potted plants on the cabin porches; these people loved flowers. The money crop overflowed into the front yard, right up to the front door of many cabins; sometimes cotton, reminding us of Texas sharecroppers; sometimes tobacco; sometimes sorghum cane. But at almost every cabin there was a row of potted flowering plants edging the front porch, the plants usually growing in one-gallon lard cans. Occasionally a discarded automobile tire was used to outline a flower bed, after about one half the width of the tire had been cut away; and that means work, as you will learn if you try to cut a tire in two, circumference-wise.

The rough roads usually had the worst bumps over the culvert at the bottom of an easy slope; we learned to cross these culverts cautiously, but not until we had paid for the lesson. For two hours we had pulled at twenty miles an hour, often in second gear. We were advised later that a combination of extra-heavy spring rains and inadequate rock bases had damaged a number of Georgia roads.

Six miles north of Waycross the engine suddenly seemed to run easier. I looked back just in time to see the trailer coming up beside us, missing the edge of the culvert by two inches, then veering into the swampy roadside ditch—again! This time the trailer had "jumped the ball." The Georgia State Highway Department has not yet sued us for breaking off the three-inch thick pine tree which brought the trailer to a sudden halt just inside the right of way.

Jerry found a farmer with a Fordson, but the trailer wouldn't budge. A modern wrecking truck arrived, with all the tackle needed for inching the trailer out of the muck. But the driver was a greenhorn and in five minutes had his own truck hopelessly mired. Another wrecker had to be called to rescue the first one. Eventually our trailer reached dry ground and the only external damage was a slight dent in the curved "bustle" at the front end; there was also a $20.00 dent in the pocketbook. Inside, things were rather a mess. The living-room carpet was well marinated with a mixture of orange juice, beer, cottage cheese, broken glass, and other remnants. The door of the refrigerator was the only one that had come open. We never mentioned this mishap when writing to the home folks—afraid someone might start calling our trailer a swamp buggy.

We hooked onto our truck; the ball joint seemed unharmed. The electrical connections were broken but a passing traveler, who said he used to work in a trailer factory, repaired them.

At Waycross the hitch was replaced with one having a stronger, more positive latch. Many miles and two months were to elapse before we had all parts of our rigging altered to our satisfaction.

Miles north of Waycross we had begun to notice the blackish color of the water in low spots, the dark water which prevails through lower Georgia and much of Florida. Somehow we had expected the Suwannee to have clear, blue water, though, on second thought, Stephen Foster had not so specified. And then we saw the origin of the Suwannee, the Okefenokee Swamp, about the color of cloudy, black tea. Waycross was the first place we noticed the sulphur smell of the water; it was rather pronounced at some of our Florida camps where we soon learned that the odor could be easily dissipated by heat. Although I scoured and scoured, one big, aluminum stewpan shows a dark line to this day.

Tall, slender pines surrounded our trailer at Waycross; brown-headed nuthatches were visible but not vocal; other birds were few. We learned that the only way to really see the big swamp was to hire a boat—and this was the wrong season, for bird recorders. Moreover, letters were waiting for us, we hoped, at Thomasville.

It was October 3, 1949, when we headed westward. In the fields along the road were broomweed and bitterweed still spreading their mantles of gold; in brushy lands the dark magenta knots of Callicarpa were familiar—we called them French mulberry in east Texas; some gardeners use the ambiguous title "beautyberry," but it is also applied to other shrubs. The wooded sections of our road contained sweet gums, tulip trees, blue gum, and some dogwood with their berries turning scarlet.

At an attractive turnout under a big pine tree we paused for lunch. Trash cans were near every table yet the ground was littered with beer cans, paper sacks, pie plates, rain-soaked cartons, broken bottles—and more beer cans. On later trips into Florida we noticed the neatness of the roadside parks and Jerry began the practice of sending a card of thanks and praise to the state highway department. Scolding careless users would do little good, even if we had an opportunity.

We recalled a roadside park in Ohio where a red-eyed vireo talked contentedly overhead while we ate our lunch at the edge of a gorge, clear water sparkling below, a columbine in bloom, a linden tree, witchhazel, and red haw nearby. At a park in Texas two scissor-tailed flycatchers displayed scarlet flanks in aerial gymnastics. In Arkansas a pileated woodpecker scouted us, peeking from behind one tree, then another, his red crest jerking quickly behind the tree trunk after each inspection. The highway workers may not realize that they also deserve praise for the wild birds seen in our roadside parks.

When we reached Thomasville, Georgia, there was nearly a bushel basketful of mail waiting for us.

The months of October through January passed swiftly at Thomasville and Tampa, with pleasant trailer-park headquarters, first in a grove of tall pines, then near a bank of the tropical Hillsborough River. We explored many state parks and wildlife refuges of the regions to find suitable spots where we could, and later did, record wild bird songs, after spring brought the birds back into more vocal mood.

Chapter IV

KELLOGGS AND THE EVERGLADES

THANKS to an introductory letter from Herbert Stoddard, noted wild-life authority, we received a cordial invitation from the Paul Kelloggs, on Sabbatical leave from Cornell University, to visit them near Miami. Leaving our trailer in Bradenton, we went bouncing down the Tamiami Trail on February 1, 1950, expecting to see the Everglades and the Keys and get some advice from the Kelloggs, all in two or three days. The Trail was more interesting than we had expected. We had known that herons and egrets and other wading birds would be common, but we hadn't realized we could get such close-up views of them. We had expected the landscape would be nothing but swamp grass for a hundred miles. But numerous cypress hammocks and a few picturesque Seminole villages, open-sided, palm-thatched shelters and women in varicolored, full-skirted costumes, some wearing their unique, black-halo headdress, gave variety and color. Possibly the women had been posed there solely to sell souvenirs and their permission for photographs. The long, narrow dugout canoes apparently were used more for posing than for real fishing. Flat-bottomed boats, powered with old automobile engines and airplane propellers, were used for conducted tours along narrow water lanes through the sea of sedge grass.

The farther south we got the better we liked the country. By the time the cordial, congenial, hospitable, knowledgeable

Kelloggs had introduced us to the new boardwalk, built to run out into a bird-filled swamp in the newly nationalized Everglades Park, we were so entranced that we started back to Bradenton, double time. We brought our trailer to the Royal Palm Trailer Park, at Homestead, only a few miles from the Kelloggs' cottage on the south campus of the University of Miami. We then expected to stay two weeks—but it stretched to six. We sent a telegram to Dorothy England, in Dallas, urging that she call our mutual friend Anne Orr, pack her movie camera, and hurry on down with Anne.

Dr. Peter Paul Kellogg was Dr. Arthur A. Allen's assistant at the Laboratory of Ornithology at Cornell. He had charge of the sound recording, while Dr. Allen specialized in photography. Kellogg had then been recording bird songs for nearly twenty years, first using movie sound film; later he recorded directly on phonograph discs. He began using tape for his sound recordings a little after we did, but he had thoroughly investigated all makes of recorders, kinds of tape, makes of microphones, and other devices useful in such projects. Jerry had hoped merely to get a few suggestions regarding our equipment and techniques but it developed that Kellogg was more than willing to check both our equipment and our recordings. It seemed to us that the equipment he had with him amounted to a complete sound laboratory.

Byrl Kellogg, a librarian by profession, was her energetic husband's assistant in any capacity he might desire, from gracious hostessing to operating a recorder—even to completing a stiff course in navigation!

The days were full at Homestead. In addition to the Tamiami Trail there were the Everglades, the Keys, marsh birds, exotic flora. As for the Miami beach where it was cluttered with rows of white skyscraper hotels, a quick spin was enough to satisfy us.

The boardwalk, built deep into the swamp near Royal Palm

Hammock, now headquarters of the Everglades National Park, is officially designated "Anhinga Trail." Our first visit was under the guidance of the Kelloggs, arriving, of course, before dawn. Great blue herons and big, white, American egrets groaned on their big bass viols. Coots clucked and cackled, blending with similar but higher-pitched calls from common and purple gallinules. White ibis flew by with rude Bronx cheers. Anhingas clacked as if their ratchet wheels were running down. I recalled Halloween memories of a notched spool spun against a window pane. As daylight increased, these marsh birds became more conscious of their vocal limitations but continued their wading, fishing, paddling, diving, flapping, posing, preening, chasing, quarreling, jostling, and low circling. They were quite indifferent to us staring, sluggish, wingless, featherless creatures standing there helpless to spear a lazy garfish or even to scoop in a minnow. Snowy egrets, Louisiana herons and little blues were common in the community. Wood ibis were the largest of the waders and especially showy in flight, the black-tipped wings contrasting with their white bodies. A sora rail was shyest but a green heron demonstrated his ability to shrink, as well as freeze, so well that I mistook him at first for a least bittern.

Next after the green jay, of Mexico and the Valley, and after our own painted bunting, I nominate the purple gallinule, with his purple and bronze body accented by the sky-blue cap and red bill tipped with yellow, as our most beautifully colored bird. They were also the most friendly birds in the swamp. If Dorothy didn't get her color movies at five feet, as we had promised, she surely got some at ten. The ranger told us that one morning when he was alone on the pier, one of them came up and pecked at the shiny buttons on his coat sleeve.

According to Jerry's version there is a story that one morning while Dr. Kellogg was recording out here, his Sigma Zi key fell into four feet of water. The purple gallinule came over, took one look at Paul's furrowed brow, dived, and returned with *three* keys, not only Sigma Zi but Tau Beta Pi and Phi Beta Kappa, which he carefully placed on a lily pad in easy reach of the worried professor. Thereafter that grateful bird recorder added another string of letters after his own name, conferred *cum laude,* in *medias res, cum grano salis.*[1]

But Dr. Kellogg tells a better one about Jerry. One morning before dawn the two men were at the Boardwalk, Paul out at the swamp end of the walk while Jerry stayed at the car to operate Paul's recorder.

"How did you like that for an alligator roar?" Paul said presently. "We must have gotten a good recording that time!"

"Alligator!" Jerry shouted back. "I thought it was a truck stuck in the mud and I stopped the recorder!"

One day we drove to the end of the old Key Road where a few charred piles mark the last of a bridge that once spanned a mile or more of dancing Atlantic waves. Mangroves lined our road. There we met our first prairie warbler, quite sophisticated with black circles under his eyes and a distinctive song, buzzy yet musical, the deliberate stairstep notes rising gently in pitch. But many a bird is more easily heard than recorded.

Another day we followed side roads bordering acres of tomatoes, quarter sections of tomatoes, until a cardinal sang, far from the trucks of the picking crews. A few of his songs got on our tape before a dusting plane appeared. On one scouting trip through the Redlands district we made a date for a porchlight connection. The next morning the recorder caught dogs and trucks and roosters along with a brown thrasher, a pair of cardinals, male and female, doing the same song by turns, a ground dove rather far away, a Florida meadowlark.

Friends helped to speed our days; Mr. and Mrs. Harry Wal-

[1] A grain of salt—on the bird's tail, no doubt.

lenburg evading another Fort Worth winter; Anne Orr and Dorothy England in Anne's new car, Dorothy with her camera and Anne with fishing rod or paint pallette. Dorothy has the sharpest eyes for birds of anyone we know. Anne is capable as many things: a lawyer, accountant, income-tax expert, fisherman, botanist, conservationist, and landscape painter. She and Dorothy stayed at a tourist court until Dorothy had to fly back to Dallas. Then Anne parked her coupe, at night, beside our trailer. She had made changes in certain seat bolts that would permit the seat back to lie flat at night to support an air mattress and sleeping bag. She refused to occupy the folding divan in our trailer.

Toe-of-the-boot! One morning we drove down beyond Royal Palm Hammock through what remained of the village of Flamingo, one tumbledown shack on stilts, occupied by an old sea captain. "The mildest mannered man that ever scuttled ship or cut a throat." He gravely assured us that the small birds feeding on his largess of yellow cornmeal were "the last survivors of the Cape Sable sparrow." After consulting a park naturalist we learned that the last of that rare subspecies was (presumably) wiped out in the "big blow" of 1935.

Down the road a way, two pileated woodpeckers were probing the rotting trunks of three lonesome palms, the only trees in sight for miles. Dorothy has them in action on several feet of film. Of all places to find a pileated woodpecker!

We drove on down to Slagles Ditch, a tidal canal about five feet wide. The bridge was gone but a fading trail went on through the marshy prairie, presumably to the tip of the toe of the boot. Slagles Ditch was suddenly lined with fishermen —the tide was coming in. Cholly, the local guide and boatman, lived here in the dry season in a tiny trailer with his pretty, part-Seminole wife. Mrs. Cholly, admitting her doubts about the identification, also fed the "Cape Sable sparrows." Dorothy photographed a few.

On the way home, we suddenly saw two big, silvery sandhill cranes in a swampy prairie, close enough for us to admire their red caps. Dorothy moved fast and got a short run before the two birds strode out of sight into a cypress hammock.

One morning Jerry and I unloaded our recording machinery at a previously scouted corner near a drainage ditch deep in the Everglades. Signs of dawn were very faint when I carried one microphone line across the ditch, crawling on hands and knees over a four-by-twelve stringer, all that remained of an old bridge, crawling because of dim light as well as a poor sense of balance. I had pulled the line about fifty yards into the clearing when I glimpsed a slinky, four-footed animal crossing the path about twenty feet in front of me. A big cat with a short tail! I dropped the microphone in the grass and arrived back at the car in something less than two seconds! Nobody knows how I got back across the drainage ditch. The bobcat probably made twice as good time in the opposite direction.

As daylight came, two blue-gray gnatcatchers fussed and sputtered within three feet of the microphone; a belted kingfisher clattered repeatedly up and down the ditch; a red-tailed hawk screamed—once. As usual in this region, electric power was not in reach and we were trying to use the converter, which was attached to the car battery and was supposed to send 120-volt alternating current to the recorder, but 90 was the best it would do. We could record fairly well with this lower voltage, but always had to pre-erase old tape before re-using it. Also there was something Jerry called "residual hum," which could be greatly reduced by providing a ground wire. This day the brass ground rod was thrust deep in the mud at the edge of the drainage ditch. The mud was as sticky as a spider's web in a greenbrier thicket in the middle of August.

When Jerry pulled the rod out he had to spend ten minutes washing off the mud. When we played back our recordings, at the trailer, every song was obscured by hum. The mud had acted as an insulator, killing the grounding effect. Yet on the sandy coastal plain of Texas it had been necessary to pour water around the rod to improve its grounding efficiency.

One evening the Wallenbergs went with us to the Boardwalk. Before dark a shower gave us *four full-circle, concentric rainbows!* The inner one was faintest. Snowy and American egrets came drifting in to roost on the trees edging the open water. The snowys were fussy, driving each other from perch to perch and spreading their beautiful nuptial plumes. It was quite dark when the wood ibis advanced in close formation from behind a bushy willow, leisurely probing the mud for their suppers. Jerry struck a match—and the entire flock rose as one bird—as though he had fired a cannon! He worried half the night about whether the birds got back safely to their swampy home.

On a trip to Key West, which included exploring side roads, we found Robert Allen of the National Audubon staff, then finishing his outstanding book about the whooping cranes. Jerry was interested in the heavy steel cables extending over each end of his garage, attached on each side to heavy "dead men," monstrous logs set deep in the earth. Bob had been through some of the "big blows" down there. He told us exactly where to find one of the rare, and localized, great white herons; we found the bird, identity confirmed by his yellow legs. Man-of-war birds hung as motionless as if painted on a canvas sky.

From the Keys the blues and greens of the shallow waters vary with depth and distances, with the angles and intensities of the sunlight and the shadows of billowy white clouds. There were patches of mauve where purple seaweed floated just below the surface. Some mountain lakes in the northwestern states show a darker blue but in no other waters have we seen such varieties of bright blues and greens. Think of Maxfield Parrish, of blue vitriol, both shades of Mexican blue glass, of opals, of a real sea-green, the color of new willow leaves seen through a fine mist, of turquoise and sapphire, of peacock plumes. There were dancing little white caps but no white sails, for a brisk breeze had brought out the red warning flag for small craft. How we treasure the little seascape, painted in oil by Anne Orr, titled "West from the Keys!" It later received honorable mention in a Dallas exhibit.

A card from Belle Wilson, a former Dallas birder, advised us to see the wonderful shells and shore birds of Florida's Sanibel Island. Taking advantage of Jerry's scheduled full day of recording technicalities with Dr. Kellogg, Anne Orr and I drove back over the Tamiami Trail to visit the island. It was the seventh of March, and the dead-looking cypress in the hammocks were coming back to life with lacy head veils of pale green. We caught the late afternoon ferry and had the thrill of spending a night on the island beach, sleeping in Anne's car. We were wakeful because of the sound of the waves, the beauty of the moonlight on the water, the novelty of the adventure—and because of some uncertainty as to the time and height of the tides. Dawn found us combing the beach but we were not ahead of an elderly couple of connoisseurs who carried light, short-handled, four-pronged rakes and very small bags in which they placed very few shells. No doubt it is experts like these who find the shells worth twenty-five dollars apiece. We neglected the shore birds because the reading glasses needed to examine shells did not combine well with binoculars. Our greatest treasure from Sanibel Island is the memory of a night on the beach.

Headquarters of Everglades National Park, called Royal Palm Hammock, or Paradise Key, is a key only in the rainy season. It has the greatest variety of native trees and shrubs to be found in southern Florida. According to Dr. J. K. Small, authority on southern flora, this 400 acres contains 162 species of flowering plants of which forty-six are trees; he listed thirteen species of ferns. He named 600 species of plants on the Florida keys, about 170 of them trees and shrubs.

Perhaps the most striking native shrub of the region is the coralbean, *Erythrina herbacea arborea*, which grows in thickets or woods throughout the gulf coastal plain. The rosy red flowers are about the size and shape of a garden pea pod; the long, dark, contorted pods split open when dry, and continue to display the scarlet beans for a year or two—if the stalks are brought indoors. Probably the popularity of these bean stalks for dried arrangements is a factor in the relative scarcity of the shrub. It seems to be particular as to soil and climate.

Park naturalists taught us to recognize the cabbage palms, or palmettos, by the fan-shaped leaves with the coarse raveling threads dangling from the undersides. They are abundant around there, but we did not try cooking one of the "cabbages." Anne would not have allowed it as this would kill the plant. Anne, friend to all small, neglected, helpless things, always stopped her car to rescue terrapins, snakes, even crabs from the highway. A prim and dainty little species we called silver palm, because of the color of the leaves. Howell mentions it in his *Birds of Florida*. Royal and coconut palms are easily recognized, but a visit to Fairchild's Gardens left our brains whirling—Nature has thought of more than 500 ways to vary the palm.

It was worthwhile for us wanderers in the wild to learn that gumbo-limbo has thin, rust-colored bark which peels in papery layers, somewhat like a river birch, while poisonwood has bark something like sycamore, flaking off in patches to show the rusty inner bark. It wasn't hard to see that the potato tree, with gray wooly leaves, white star flowers, and little, yellow tomato fruits, belongs to the nightshade family, along with tomatoes and potatoes. Strangler figs, or banyan trees, surround and smother nearby trees by roots sent down from the branches.

Anne and I spent a morning at the University of Florida subtropical experiment station, near Homestead, under the generous guidance of Mr. Robert G. Newcomb, an agronomist of the staff. We came home babbling about loquats with the color and texture of apricots, the size and form of crab apples; of tamarind, or "Indian dates," the pulp more tart than real dates; of fragrant, sweet carambolas; of star apples with yellow flesh, the "star" visible in cross section; of natal plums (*Carissa grandiflora*) with fruits resembling red raspberries in flavor and color (Bailey's encyclopedia compares them to cranberries); of other tropicals so numerous we had worn out our tasters and our notebook pencils.

Papayas were common around Homestead; their juicy, cantaloupelike fruits became a part of the daily menu. Sea-grape jelly, light pink in color, tasted rather like the familiar apple-quince combination. "Rich are the pomegranates," but when friends wrote that redbud and dogwood were in bloom in Dallas, we felt a pang for the carpet of trout lilies, like spring snowdrifts, in the woods at Ellowi, the Camp Fire Girls' camp southwest of Dallas. We used to pick a small bouquet of them in order to catch their delicate fragrance.

Bird recording was completely fascinating but we only pretended that we never got homesick. Both of us, together, in this foreign land, remembered the lines from T. A. Daly's *Mona Machree:*

> *This, the new goddess to whom I'm beholden*
> *Snares me in days that are scented and golden.*
> *Far to the south and far to the (east) of you,*
> *Rich are the pomegranates, luscious and sweet—*
> *But oh the red lips of you, Mona Machree!*

Daly's little book of verse was the first gift I ever received from Jerry. But our love of poetry was second to our love of birds.

Dr. Kellogg, with a keen understanding of human as well as electronic characteristics, used tact as well as technical skill in his attack upon our recording problems. He tackled the converter and checked the filter; then a minor surgical operation was performed for the insertion of a rheostat to control field current, which controls rotor speed, which controls cycles, and therefore pitch accuracy. The rheostat came by airmail from Chicago; Kellogg found a "surplus" cycle meter. All connecting lines between converter, Jerry's control box, and the recorder were oriented and connection plugs then marked with red fingernail polish; provision was made for a better grounding terminal.

At odd moments, to fill in time not spent on his own bird recording or given to the likes of us, Kellogg dusted off his sextant and gave instructions in navigation aboard a craft of the Miami power squadron.

Jerry could match the younger fellow in enthusiasm and patience and he had one advantage in that he could give all of his time to his hobby. Leisure can be the blessing or the curse of retired folks. Lucky are they who discover how to spend it! We were lucky—lucky in friendships too.

Although we did get a few passable records with the converter power, the net result was the conclusion that this six-volt converter could not give really dependable results in our work. Then the recorder was uncased, its innermost thoughts explored with some sort of lie detector called an oscilloscope. Our teacher's standards were high; finally he told us frankly that our efforts warranted a better recorder. Mixed in with Jerry's six weeks of basic training were demonstrations on splicing mediums and splicing templates; discussions on paperback versus plastic tape; seven and one-half inch speed versus fifteen inch per second for bird recording. We were converted to all the quality-improving changes, but our first recorder would run only at seven and one-half inch speed. There were demonstrations of the proper techniques in preparing and soldering mike-line connections, on the advantages of pre-amplifiers and parabolic reflectors, and, like the farmer's bill of sale, many other items too numerous to mention. At long last decibels had been added to our vocabulary, incorporated into our very breathing. Having observed the type of line connector used by Kellogg, Jerry secured a supply and replaced the clumsier type originally furnished by a Dallas man. The old connectors were deposited in an ash can and Jerry oozed smugness until, months later, a radio-station engineer in Louisville, Kentucky, uncovered a miscue in conductor orientation in Jerry's part of the work.

The low-voltage trouble, when recording, was banished permanently by the purchase of a voltmeter and a manually controlled, variable-output, isolation transformer whereby an incoming voltage of 100 or less could be boosted to the 120 value needed by our recorder. They gave yeoman service. Another purchase was a line filter, which seemed to function properly for a while, then seemed reluctant, and finally was deposited with care in a handy junk pile.

Gradually our plans were formulated: we'd drift north, taking our time and recording on the way; find a suitable place to spend about three weeks where jobbers and technicians could be found, as well as some worthwhile birds; reorganize and upgrade some of our equipment; then on north for that hermit thrush. Louisville, Kentucky, was selected as our base, letters were written, and the way was charted. As might be expected, some changes were made in our routings, and more time than expected was required before we approached the goal that Dr. Kellogg had inspired.

Near Sebring, in central Florida, we visited the Archbold

Biological Station, thirty miles off the main road. We arrived at dawn; no one was in sight. Jerry found an electrical connection and our recorder was ready for action. Here we found elusive Florida jays. By sunup they were eating grain from our hands; they perched on the recorder; one lit on my hat—but they *said* very little. A visiting scientist from Utah stood back of us and exposed two rolls of Kodachrome. Humph! Photographers' birds!

At last the birds deserted us. We looked up to find another man standing behind us, a big man with black, bushy hair—and a kindly twinkle in his eyes. Dr. Archbold made us welcome, showed us around some of his thousand-acre reserve and through the commodious laboratories and study rooms. He had tried to record birds on movie film to get both songs and photographs at the same time. Even his equipment of superb photographic lenses could not overcome all the difficulties. One of the best places for photography of small birds is at the nest, the very place where the bird is least likely to sing.

The Archbold Station was popular with a number of biologists who pursued their researches in a most congenial environment. Dr. James G. Needham was there, completing a revision of his book on dragonflies. We first met this famous entomologist, and master of belles-lettres, in Dallas years ago. Although he had celebrated his eighty-second birthday, his mind was as keen as ever. We felt the old fascination as he spent an hour describing some of his recent discoveries. We had appreciated, long ago, the magic of his personality and the breadth of his purpose, a magic which has long pervaded the biology faculty at Cornell.

Cornell University was the founding home of the "nature study idea" as propounded by Anna Botsford Comstock, and continued by such famous personalities as Liberty Hyde Bailey (*Encyclopedia of Horticulture*), Dr. Needham, Dr.

E. L. Palmer of *Rural School Leaflet* and *Nature Magazine* fame, and Drs. Arthur A. Allen and Peter Paul Kellogg with their bird pictures and songs. These naturalists have not only extended scientific knowledge in their spheres, but also succeeded in interesting a wide public, as well as their students, in the *aesthetic* and *recreational* values of nature lore. Some conservationists act as if nature preservation must be advocated on a commercial basis. The Cornell biologist and the National Audubon Society represent two of the country's best hopes for stimulating a *wide* appreciation of our *natural* assets.

Chapter V

OTTER CREEK PARK

A LETTER outlining our interest in birds had been sent to Burt Monroe, who lived in a suburb of Louisville, and, as a long-time national officer of the Wilson (ornithological) Club, could be depended on to know bird haunts in his vicinity. He suggested Otter Creek Park, an area used for organizational camping, twenty-five miles from Louisville. We were to ask for Clinton Johnson.

We'd have to push along if we hoped to reach Louisville with the warblers. So May Day was moving day. Flat lands were behind us; the red hills of Alabama lay ahead. There were more wild flowers than we had seen since we left Texas. Yellow coreopsis and the small, deep lavender verbenas were plentiful. The tall, white Baptisia, sister of the blue wild indigo and the yellow goatweeds of east Texas, was showy. There were many flowering shrubs: pink and white azaleas, blackberries, elderberries, huckleberries, some delicately tinted with pink; also fringe trees, a little red honeysuckle, crab apple, two kinds of magnolias as well as tulip trees with their yellow cups. The white and pink-tinted rain lilies, Zephyranthes, were half as big as Easter lilies. Crimson clover overflowed from fields to brighten and enrich the roadsides. All along the way dogwood was in bloom. Haven't you dreamed of traveling north in the spring, keeping pace with dogwood and redstarts?

Contour terracing was not enough to hold the steep slopes

of red clay and sand in Alabama; a Negro following a one-horse plough, his unpainted shack in the background, was working his cotton field. Judging by the signs of erosion, more of the slopes might better have been given back to the pine trees.

Northward the native flora gradually shifted from east Texan to Ozarkian: dogwood and azaleas continued among the pines, soon were varied with the new green of oaks and maples. Mayapples and woods phlox were joined by the dingy lavender of bouncing Betty, by crowfoot violets, pale purple but especially conspicuous because the many plants were crowded with long-stemmed flowers. In the fields appeared oxeye daisies and a new thistle, wine-red and very prickly, a scarlet fire-pink, and, in the towns, lilacs and snowballs. The blue-lavender, catalpalike flowers, of naturalized Paulownia trees were more showy against the dark pines than against the blue sky.

Clouds grew almost as black as the asphalt road and soon blinding rain forced us to pause at the first wide spot beside the road. We found ourselves parked beside a combination grocery, hardware store, and filling station. Four house trailers were parked on the crowded platform. The proprietor advised us that there was no other trailer camp for at least twenty-five miles. Since more black clouds threatened we decided to stay for the night and were assigned a narrow space just back of the store. Here a van freighter noisily unloaded hardware at 2 A.M. We were ready to leave at the first sign of dawn. The only way we could get out was straight ahead, down a steep, trailer-scraping driveway into a narrow street. Six miles down the road we passed a fine, roomy trailer park with big shade trees.

As we neared our goal we ignored all distractions and kept to the charted route. The big TVA dam across the Cumberland River was bypassed, though only a few miles out of our way. Pulaski, Tennessee, was, to us, only a broken front spring. Nashville had the steepest city street we ever saw on a through-truck-traffic route. We drove through Bowling Green on the day before Derby Day without even seeing a horse. Since we had seen Carlsbad we ignored Mammoth Cave. We began to look for the turnoff that was to lead us to Otter Creek Park.

Near the village of Westpoint, on our side road, we began the descent into a beautiful little valley. Then, after crossing a clear, purling stream, we climbed a long, steep hill and found the sign: HEADQUARTERS, OTTER CREEK PARK.

A workman took us in his pickup truck a mile through woods and meadows to a group of rustic cabins. Clinton Johnson was finishing his lunch, sitting under a massive oak tree. Mrs. Johnson was sketching dogwood blossoms. Both of them are landscape architects; he was formerly with the U. S. Forest service. Both are versatile, talented, and friendly; they love trees and wild flowers and wanted to know more about birds. Fate had pulled the puppet strings again and this time set the stage for one of the most enjoyable summers ever experienced by this pair of bird recorders.

We were back at the park headquarters with the trailer in location by 4 P.M., all set, dog-tired, in bed by 7 P.M. At eight o'clock I nudged Jerry:

"There's a whippoorwill calling!"

The microphones and wires were in the truck. Jerry bounced out the door, clad only in undershorts and slippers. By the time the recorder was in operation the whippoorwill had moved a little, but his voice got on the tape. After weeks of growing friendship the Johnsons told us the joke. They, now "Clint and Olivia," had been working in the office that first evening and had watched our proceedings.

Our whippoorwill's singing territory covered an area with a radius of about one-fourth mile and his routine was soon discovered. He sang quite regularly, every evening between eight and eight-thirty and again in the morning between four-thirty and five, from the roof of a low shed about thirty feet from the trailer. First we'd hear him from a distance, then from the shed roof. On many of these mornings and evenings, using an improvised tackle, a microphone was hoisted to the roof comb to a position about two feet from his preferred singing perch.

The whip has a strong voice and the three-note song can be heard for three-eighths mile or more. At a distance of fifty feet a fourth note may be heard, something like the syllable "tuck," which precedes the "whip" by about six-hundredths of a second. This was the first bird from which we'd ever heard the tuck sound, although it is well known and has been heard by many people. Many have also noted the regularity and long continuity of the bird's songs, which, with some odd exceptions, are repeated at the rate of once every second. One observer timed the bird with a metronome for 900 repetitions.

At least once during each morning and evening singing period near us, the bird uttered another low-voiced call, inaudible at more than fifteen feet, something like "gaw gaw gaw gaw. . . ." The pitch of this sound was at least an octave below the pitch of the lowest note in his regular song. Always, with our bird, the gaw call was preceded by a doubling in tempo of his regular song, that is to two "whip-poor-wills" per second. Bent, in his famous *Life Histories of Birds*, quotes Bendire, who describes a call, possibly this one, heard at very close range, uttered by a female. Bendire considered the call as a mating or courtship manifestation.

Louisville's Otter Creek Park embraces some 2000 acres of wooded hills bordering the Ohio River and was developed by the National Park Service during the old WPA depression days. In addition to camping and picnic grounds, and two lodges for small groups, there are three well-developed sites for large, organized groups, each unit containing a mess hall, recreation halls, and detached sleeping cabins. The units are rented, during the summer months, to Boy Scouts, Y.M.C.A., Y.W.C.A., church groups, and the like. The headquarters area, where our trailer was located, included office, garage, workshops, and storage sheds. Some fifteen workmen were employed in maintenance and construction. In addition to supervising them, the director served as arbitrator of minor difficulties in campers' affairs, as chief police officer enforcing the conservation of all forms of wildlife, as purchasing agent, bookkeeper, payroll and budget director. He worked with a three-man governing commission appointed by the city of Louisville. Twice during our stay Johnson was called out, late at night, to solve a who-dun-it at one of the camps. Mysterious sounds were involved which later were discovered to be the mischievous pranks of some youngsters who sought to mystify a lady counselor.

Late in the summer we prepared a special reel of songs we had recorded at Otter Creek; we called it "The Commissioners' Reel." Clint brought them to the trailer one day to hear it. Maybe they liked it. At any rate it was after this that Jerry was invited to play some of his bird songs at a television interview on one of the local stations. All went well on that occasion until the last, when Jerry called for the song of the brown thrasher and the disc jockey produced the song of the orchard oriole! Probably I was the only one who noticed the mistake for Jerry was too excited, and no listeners offered a correction.

In addition to recording bird songs while at Otter Creek, we made several purchases to improve our equipment, a result of the encouragement and advice from Dr. Kellogg. We procured a combination preamplifier and switch box, a parabolic reflector, a new recording machine, and, finally, a converter, for mobile power whenever electric lines would not be in reach. We expected to obtain the four pieces of equipment within two or three weeks. It took all summer.

During the first month we went to town, "Loovil," every other day on errands connected with one phase or another of our recording needs. Jerry had discussed his preamplifier and switch box needs with various technical experts prior to reaching Louisville and had been told that his ideas were not feasible. Here, thanks to Clinton Johnson's introduction, he met Mr. Towner, chief engineer of radio station WHAS, who enlisted the aid of Ed Devine, one of his staff engineers. Jerry gave Mr. Devine an outline of how he wanted to use the devices and the results desired. Devine asked for a few days to study the matter. On our next visit he said he had located a ready-built switch box that would do part of the job; he designed and built the auxiliary equipment to meet our full needs.

The new gadgets included: input connections for five microphones, with snap switches permitting the monitoring of signals from all at once or from each separately; amplification of sound and control of volume, with its own vu meter; in-and-out impedances matching our equipment. The two car-battery-sized boxes comprising the unit were designed for either battery or house current and could be used either near the recorder or near a field microphone. The equipment was completed exactly as Jerry desired and delivered on June 24. Similar appliances are now listed in catalogues.

While we were still in Thomasville Jerry had requested that the parabolic reflector be sent to us in care of Mr. Burt Monroe. At that time we did not know that his suburban town of Anchorage was some fifty miles from Otter Creek Park.

Burt L. Monroe worked forty hours a week at a bread-and-butter job as planning engineer for a large insurance company. He served for years as chairman of the membership committee of the nation-wide Wilson Ornithological Club, four years as treasurer of the organization, then as vice-president. He had served as president of the Kentucky Ornithological Society, and of the League of Kentucky Sportsmen. He still wrote a weekly outdoor column for a local newspaper. He was official state ornithologist for the state of Kentucky. Apparently, in his spare time on Sundays, he just puttered in his garden.

On Monroe's first visit to us at Otter Creek he took us to "The Landing," the once flourishing river port of Rock Haven. Here a Baltimore oriole sang from the topmost branch of a cottonwood tree. Everywhere we went the Baltimores seemed to prefer cottonwoods. On his second visit he was beaming when he unloaded the reflector from his car; he had besieged the Express office every day for a week or more before he found our package, overlooked behind a mass of other objects.

The reflector was an aluminum saucer, thirty inches in diameter, called "parabolic" because its curvature was so designed that the sound waves (light waves would act the same) reflected from its surface were brought to a focus. In ours the focus was some ten inches in front of the center. By attaching the microphone at this point, facing the reflector of course, the volume of sound was multiplied four or five times, as if the bird were that much closer. The reflector also tended to shut out unwanted sounds behind it or at the sides. The principal difficulty I had in using it was in getting it aimed rather accurately at the wanted bird. Jerry bored a small peephole near the center of focus to improve my aim. There was more scurrying around town to find a tripod and then a machine shop to cast and turn the fittings needed to permit swinging the reflector in almost any direction.

On another trip Burt Monroe brought Basil Doehoeffer out for a visit to show us Basil's trained falcon; one look at the beak and talons was enough to explain the need for specially made, heavy, alligator gloves. The bird had the fierce but gentle look in his eyes that may be observed in some of Fuertes paintings of African hawks.

A few days after reaching the vicinity of Louisville we had

begun to shop for a new tape recorder. We knew what we would like to have, one just like Dr. Kellogg's: a three-piece Presto with snap-switch changeover between seven and one-half and fifteen-inch speed, an immediate-playback head whereby one could listen to the recording about two-sevenths of a second after it was recorded, a dial vu meter for registering the volume of sound. We had been told that deliveries were slow on that model. After we had ordered it days passed; weeks passed. The salesman said he had written and wired the factory. Still no results. Then came a letter from Kellogg saying a recorder of the kind we wanted had just arrived in Miami and he could get it for us with an educational discount. We sent him the check by air mail, suggesting that he try for an extra 2 per cent discount for cash and use it to buy beer. He got the 2 per cent and used it to buy the best recording tape —for us.

There was no Express station at Rock Haven. It was said that, in the days when steamboats on the Ohio River furnished the only way a lady of quality should travel, Rock Haven had been a port of some importance. Nowadays the steamboats had been replaced by tugs pushing strings of barges loaded with coal, or brick, or automobiles; railroad trains did not stop; incoming mail was tossed onto a platform; outgoing mail was snatched from a post. Our nearest Express office was an "open-maybe" station called Brandenburg.

On our third trip the new recorder had arrived. Apparently the big package had been handled carelessly since some small parts seemed slightly damaged. After Jerry had made repairs he found the assistant chief engineer of a radio station who used a recorder like ours and agreed to check it for us. He worked all of a Saturday afternoon checking every point and pronounced it in perfect condition. At long last we had a recorder that knew its business and with some gadgets that would tell us whether it was lying.

Then, with the reflector, we got more wood thrush; some of the bird is on our first LP disc. We even recorded him simultaneously with the music from a phonograph record. The mike where the bird sang was 400 feet deep in the timber; the phonograph was in the trailer. Our new machine had three mike input sockets, the signal from each individually controllable with its own "pot"—an engineer called it the attenuator.

Another day came a letter from the converter man: he'd have to make tests with a recorder like ours before he could recommend a converter that would meet our needs. We relaxed; it was by then rather late to start on north for the hermit thrush—he would have to be postponed to another spring. In the meantime we still had bird songs every morning and the good company of the Johnsons almost every evening. Their home was just up the hill.

Conditions permitting, we recorded bird songs every morning from four-thirty to seven, although there were many interruptions even that early June was a rainy month; sometimes it was windy; often squadrons of four-motor bombers from nearby Fort Knox would fill the sky and we would have to wait until they had passed over. Often we could record directly from the trailer, sometimes from one of the lodges or camps, when temporarily free of occupants.

One morning an orchard oriole sang near the trailer, an immature male, all yellow except the black chin. He hung around for three days and before he left gave us one of the best orchard oriole songs we'd ever heard, although a full-plumaged male did a little better at Fayetteville, Arkansas, in 1951. Both birds got on our first LP disc.

Hours were spent trying for a chipping sparrow that sang around the trailer; his simple trill, or rattle, seemed especially hard to focus and record without distortion. I opined that the bird was an extra-poor singer and he did have a less musical quality than the bird by the postmaster's cabin. Two of the elfin, rusty-capped birds ate grain and crumbs at our doorstep more fearlessly every day, sharing the provender with a chipmunk. All drank from our bird bath, which was improvised from a kettle lid lined with newspapers so the birds would not find it slippery. But all refused to "chip" their thanks into our microphone. A few days before our departure from Otter Creek the treetop chipping sparrow relented—or I got a better aim—and we taped a fair recording of the bird. Jerry called it our "thousand-dollar bird song," for it had required all the virtues of our new equipment.

We lived high at Otter Creek. At the little country store we bought milk at sixteen cents a quart, cream too thick to pour at fourteen cents a half pint, eggs thirty cents, real country butter fifty cents. Every few days Olivia Johnson would appear at the trailer with a batch of sweet corn or tomatoes or lettuce or onions from her little garden patch.

For a time the annoyance of delays in new equipment was aggravated by microphone failures. Beginning about the time we left Thomasville, four microphones went down in quick succession. Each was forwarded to its manufacturer for repairs —and one day we were down to two usable mikes. A distributor gave us a new make for trial; we used it briefly, then traded it for a better kind—which reached us some time later. An airmail letter was sent to Kennedy England in Dallas. A week later two of the preferred makes arrived by airmail; Kenny must have used some influence in finding them for it turned out that model was temporarily out of stock at the factory during a changeover period. In another week or so we were again a nine-microphone family!

Robins hatched four youngsters twenty feet from our trailer—with no singing nearby. Later we managed to catch a little robin song while a new nest was under construction below the overhanging roof of the office. A pair of blue-gray gnatcatchers built a nest in a beautiful white oak shading the office. The nest was mortised with cobwebs and camouflaged with lichens. Efforts to catch the birds' weak, querulous voices were in vain. The nest was pointed out to Harvey Lovell when he and his companions made their breeding-bird census for *Audubon Field Notes*. This species destroys his lovely nest soon after the fledglings leave it.

Yellow-breasted chats alternately jeered and played tag with us. Maryland yellowthroats seemed to be will-o-the-wisps; goldfinches were as aimless as wandering butterflies. For a week the catbird's only vocal effort was a poor imitation of a poor white-eyed vireo song. Finally the catbird sang for an hour from the top of a small locust tree near the trailer—while the recording wheels continued to turn.

One bird-favored spot was a low thicket at the edge of the woods back of our trailer. Blackberry canes and greenbrier helped to make it impenetrable. Morning after morning we guessed wrong, moving all around the thicket, trying to focus on the yellowthroat. Several bobwhites blundered into our range one morning and one gave a call we had never heard before, the "caterwaul," appropriately so named by Stoddard, as we learned in the fall, after our stored books reached us.

We had met our first prairie warbler on the old, mangrove-lined road south of Homestead, heard them climbing their vocal stairways, though not zipping up and stumbling on the top step as parula warblers do. I did notice that the bird of this thicket seemed to run, not walk, up his vocal chromatic scale. Finally Jerry managed to pull four different mike lines into the brush and tangles. I also tried again to focus on the uphill singer. After running the recorder for about four hours we were able to salvage a total of about thirteen repetitions, all alike and not too obscured by noise. Jerry was about to file the tape under "prairie warbler" when my memory suddenly began to function. I was usually responsible for identifying the singers, not because I knew them any better, but because I was usually the fieldman while Jerry operated the recorder; also because my hearing was a little better than his. We got out the Michigan recording for comparison—and had to admit that we had recorded another field sparrow instead of a prairie warbler! The qualities of the voices are quite different, but the distance had played tricks in causing me to confuse the songs. I found what consolation I could in the fact that I had caught my own mistake.

On rainy days Jerry worked on the splicing problem. When we began recording, the manufacturers were recommending that ordinary Scotch "stickum" tape be used for splicing. A year later they produced a special splicing tape, No. 41, but Jerry did not buy it at first, as the price was too high and the width did not suit him. By now we had accumulated reels and reels of bird songs as well as recorded music. Probably no other sound-tape user has to do as much splicing as a bird recorder—and those cellophane splices were causing trouble; they oozed and they stretched and they stuck to the next layer of tape, often causing breaks. Sometimes the oxide coating would separate from the backing. Now we went through reel after reel, replacing old splices with the improved No. 41 splicing tape. Much torn tape had to be thrown away. It was months before the job of replacing old splices was completed.

The lodge called Lone Acres was on the bluff high above the Ohio River, back from the bluff edge just far enough so that we could not hear the put-put of fishermen's motor boats, far enough from the graveled road leading to the landing to escape the sound of trucks. One morning the entire Stillwell force was on the site at 4 A.M. We pulled 500 feet of power line to the lodge and ran out five mike lines. While pulling one line over logs and through bushes, I heard twigs snapping in front of me in the black woods and hoped to shine the eyes of a deer; daylight revealed only a stolid groundhog.

Stars were fading when the first performer took the stage —a cardinal giving a fine song which we had not heard before —or since. Our mike line in his direction was 500 feet long— he sang 200 feet farther west. We did not get that cardinal song, a sixty-second burst of melody which made us feel he could have been a logical contender for the honored place in our memories held by a cardinal near the bus station in Lake Charles, Louisiana. Next, at the opposite end of the wooded lane, a Carolina wren gave a dozen repetitions of a good song, nicely recorded. Third of the day was an indigo bunting, properly positioned and singing one of the best songs we had yet heard from the species. He was accompanied, at times, by a red-eyed towhee; the towhee was restless and most of his song was wasted, as far as posterity is concerned. The sun was above the horizon when a Kentucky warbler came close enough for me to catch him in the reflector-mike. The song of the Kentucky warbler resembles one of the two-note songs of the Carolina wren. The Kentucky's song consists of couplets repeated about six times, one note of each pair more heavily accented than the other. The Carolina's song usually is repeated only three or four times between pauses.

A wood thrush was singing near the lodge, over 200 feet away but focusable in the reflector and his song was taped. This was the second wood thrush we had recorded that used just four phrases over and over in the same order; the other had been at Thomasville. Soon after the Kentucky warbler departed a red-eyed vireo began singing south of us, close enough for me to follow him with the reflector; about the time he moved out of range another red-eyed vireo began to the north; this bird sang only about half as fast as the first one. At seven o'clock we heard, faintly, the voices of children at Camp Piomingo, more than a half mile away. By eight the

breeze had freshened and the memorable morning was over—
but not all over until we had reeled in nearly 2000 feet of wire
and loaded it back into the truck. Thanks largely to the new
equipment, this was the most successful recording day we had
ever had—on July 12, 1950, climaxing our third recording
season. Bird singing fades out rapidly in July.

Dogwood blossoms had been in their prime when we arrived at Otter Creek in early May. There we saw our first pink
dogwood growing in the wild. As the days slipped by, ravines
and roadsides were whitened with blackberry blossoms. Wild
blackberries probably supply more bird food than any other
fruit in our temperate zone. As the season progressed there
were wild roses, elderberry blossoms, common honeysuckle
filling the air with perfumes. Catalpa trees bloomed; orange
milkweed, daisies, fleabanes, clovers, and meadow rues, like
creamy lace, took their turns. We learned that "pink Texas
star" (rose gentian) is not confined to Texas.

In August the drooping clusters of wild black cherries began turning from red to black; every sassafras bush put on a
few scarlet mittens; Queen Anne's lace dried and curled up
to become "birds' nests"; sunflowers, rosinweeds, black-eyed
Susans; large, creamy clusters of Aralia, or Hercules club—a
fine parade of wild flowers from May through August!

On August 23 Clint Johnson went to the post office and
came back carrying a heavy parcel and wearing a long face,
as he contemplated our departure. The converter had arrived.
Of course by this time the hermit thrush was "out" for the
year. Our thought was to pull southwest. Maybe we'd stop in
Dallas long enough to install the converter in the truck and
to visit relatives and friends. Maybe we'd drift on toward
Phoenix. Time's awasting—we'd leave tomorrow. I went up to
the cottage to tell Olivia.

Clint came early to say good-by; he had a conference in
Louisville with his commissioners. A man would stay at head-

quarters to help us if needed. Before today Jerry had spent a week worrying about how much tinkering would be required to get the trailer out of mothballs and rolling again after nearly four months in one spot. Our spirits rose with the sun as each point was checked and found in order. Jerry pulled once around the flat ground at headquarters. It had been hard to tell Olivia good-by. How we treasure the watercolor of dogwood blossoms, painted especially for us, and the table runners, samples of her own artistic hand-weaving! They remind us of many happy evenings spent in the Johnson home.

After we left Otter Creek Park a few clumps of Joe-pye weed began to appear in roadside ditches and swamps; a better name is "queen-of-the-meadow," for there is something regal about their huge, flat clusters; the color is not royal purple, however, but more of a raspberry-cream. In addition to ironweed, Joe-pye has numerous lowly cousins with flower clusters like oyster-white lace, such as several bonesets and dog fennel, one with a perfume like one of the goldenrods, although a trifle sneezy. Other cousins are the pinkish climbing hempweed, with heart-shaped leaves, and blue mistflower or "wild ageratum."

Sumacs were beginning to turn red. Fruit clusters of the staghorn variety were darkest red and most compact; smooth sumac fruits, with smooth twigs in contrast to the fuzzy staghorn, are intermediate in size. Winged sumac, some still in bloom, had the largest, loosest clusters; the "wings" are leafy borders along the stem between the pairs of leaflets. Elderberry branches drooped with the weight of their glossy, purple-black fruits.

A light shower caught us at Clarksville, Tennessee. We parked behind a filling station for the night, learned that we had just passed through the most extensive burley-tobacco region in the world.

The headlines looked bad; we began to worry about the

Korean situation; gas and tire rationing might find us stuck in some part of the country where we didn't want to remain indefinitely.

Showers again until noon, but we plodded along, took to the hills. In the Ozarks, Dad (the judge) would have called the route we followed "a good, ridge road." This one had sharp curves, short, steep rises, and dips through a heavily timbered region where we could hardly see beyond the roadside, especially through the mist and rain. We drove twenty-five miles, mostly in second gear. Total wildlife: one crow. We crossed a mile-long bridge over the dammed Tennessee, here called "Kentucky Lake"; the dam was south of Paducah.

Barn swallows were migrating. A shrubby swamp plant, wild hibiscus, or rose mallow, bore showy flowers, one kind white with a crimson eye, others pale pink; they are related to cotton, okra, and hollyhocks, evident by the form of the flowers. Common evening primroses looked weedy at this season; although still blooming, the yellow flowers had gotten smaller as the season advanced, and the drying seed pods looked untidy. Cutleaf Silphium, a yellow, sunflowerlike, coarse, rough weed, has tough leaves which, as dry survivors in winter, resemble leaves of white oak. The many-branched, pale-pink Gauras made pretty ruffles on the outskirts of the highways. Purple loosestrife is really a magenta pink; Gerardias wore their ruffled flower thimbles, some pink, others yellow. Marsh fleabane was a paler purple than ironweed; many yellow-flowered bitterweeds threatened the flavor of milk from browsing cows.

We began to think out loud. "Korea may get serious. We'd better start looking for a place to hole up for the duration. Mena or Fayetteville in Arkansas? Neosho, Missouri?" We had once dreamed about spending our retirement years in the Ozarks. But of course this would not be a real retirement, just an interlude.

Memphis and evening traffic were approaching. We found a trailer park at the eastern edge of the city. Next morning we were glad to be driving through the industrial district at 6 A.M. instead of 5 P.M. Sky bright and clear; wide boulevards, immense oaks, a big, lovely park, fine old mansions. West of the city we crossed the Mississippi on a highway four lanes wide. The river serves as a moat to protect the Effete East from the Wild West.

The highway man in Little Rock mentioned 8 per cent grades in Hot Springs. We were no longer afraid of them, but they were no picnic; we decided to follow the Arkansas River valley. Neosho, Missouri, was ruled out as our future home when we remembered that a big army camp had been established nearby; that would imply many airplanes. We agreed to look around Fayetteville, Arkansas, first. Jerry had taught engineering subjects one year at the university there, some twenty-seven years ago. If nothing suited us there we'd try the Mena region to the south.

The Arkansaw Traveler park at Mountainburg looked inviting. There the Camerons had an attractive antique shop; we chose a site close to the well-named Clear Creek; blue Ozark hills rose on three sides. We were glad to park here after a mile-long descent from a ridge of the Boston Mountains, highest in the state.

We worked for an hour getting the trailer into the selected spot among the trees. Sometimes the gods take pity on us erring mortals: we were in the truck, ready for a run to a grocery store when Jerry looked back and noticed the dead tree. We delayed the start of our shopping trip while he shifted the trailer a dozen feet. When we returned the tree was down; it had missed the trailer by five feet.

We outlined our wants to a real estate agent: a small, modern, well-built house, at least one mile away from a paved highway. Unpaved roads in that region have so much natural gravel that they are passable in nearly all weather. We wanted to get away from traffic noises. We were shown termite-riddled, warped old shacks, almost ready for propping poles; a good house on top of a hill with a driveway having 10 per cent grades. One place had a 10,000-capacity brooder house, but we were not interested in the broiler business. After a few days we found just what we wanted. The place was a ten-acre wooded plot six miles from town, two miles from the paved road. The four-room rock house was nearly new. There was a stairway to the floored attic with two full-length windows in each end. The small rock structure near the back door was not what it seemed, but served as a pump house for the deep well. There was a huge garage with plenty of room for Jerry to tinker. A bulldozed "tank," or little pond, offered a prospect of bullfrogs. Some of the bird songs on our first LP record supplied the proof.

Papers were signed on September 5; we drove to Dallas for money and returned with the truck loaded with a miscellany, including a Sears eight-inch buzz saw and a shaper. There was some delay in collecting our loaned antiques and stored pieces. We continued to live in the trailer, in our own backyard, sanding floors, painting, etc. We moved into the house on November 24. The house trailer would still be used on two- or three-month spring trips for bird recording—we thought. This was *not* the end of the Bluebird Trail! Considering all the improvements in our recording equipment and the consequent vast improvement in the quality of our bird recordings, it would be more like a new beginning.

Chapter VI

AVIAN ECHOES[1]

B Y going south in March, although March winds were
quite persistent wherever we tried, and north in May and
June, even into early July, we could manage to prolong the
bird-song season only a few weeks. Therefore, for at least seven
months of the year, we told ourselves, we might as well be
comfortable in a home of our own where we could have all our
books in reach. There we could relax in our easy chairs and
have plenty of room for the limitless job of editing bird songs.
It required nearly a third of the living room and time without
end. Falls and winters would be spent in our new home, recording radio music and saving pennies for travel when birds
would be in full song.

Whenever bird recordings were of a quality worth saving,
each species was filed on a separate reel along with data on
time and place of recording. Thorough comparisons were
made with previous recordings. Although we made no scientific use of the device, we had some pleasure listening to records in slow motion; cutting tape speed to one half reduces
the pitch one octave and often produces interesting, sometimes beautiful results, although the songs are often unrecog-
nizable. Not only are some bird notes too high-pitched, at
normal speed, to be heard easily, but some are inaudible be-

[1] The best of our successful recordings of bird songs mentioned in this chapter
appear on our first LP record.

87

cause they are of such short duration. We discovered that a few bird notes seem to be double, two pitches sung at the same time! There was a Negro boy in my home town who could whistle that way, and Jerry claimed that he once had this special skill.

Combining some of our favorite bird songs with recorded classical music was another winter pastime. Conventional harmonies in pitch were rare, and accidental, yet some of our combinations sounded more harmonious to us than some of the ultramodern "serious" music. We did not have the elaborate equipment which would be necessary to fit the bird's rhythm and pitch exactly to the music. About all we could do was try many different combinations until we found some we liked. A matching of moods, we called it. Some of our friends liked the results very well—and some preferred their Schubert straight.

Texas friends, like true Texans, asked, "Why did you choose to settle down in Arkansas instead of Texas?" We couldn't think of going back to Dallas, where motor traffic and airplanes are much too noisy for really good bird recording, as is true for the environs of any city. We had spent many camping vacations in the Ozarks during the early years of our marriage and we'd always admired the variety of big trees, the hills and the rills and the wild flowers as well as the birds. This location was reasonably close to the geographical center of the country and had an equitable balance of the four seasons. We remembered long sprays of wild roses, pink ones and white, leaning over the banks of Flint Creek with its sparkling, clear, cold water. And a certain wooded ravine with a trickling waterfall—we called it Strawberry Glen; a certain wild crab-apple tree with rose and white petals and a cinnamon-and-heaven perfume, below it a carpet of little pansy-violets. Of course nobody ever tried to recapture his youth without meeting some disappointments. Now, we couldn't find Strawberry

Glen because of highway changes; the special crab-apple tree was gone; the wild roses were not as big as Cherokee roses; and Flint Creek was shrunken and not as sparkling as we remembered.

Avian Echoes was not a farm, to us. The rather small broiler house and the cowshed remained empty; we even gave away the dog kennel; weeds took over the old strawberry bed and the garden patch. But how the goldfinches reveled in the resulting weed patch! Many of the shade trees around the house were native oaks, post and blackjack and southern red. A huge, wild cherry tree and a spreading American elm grew in the pasture next to our place. We planted more wild roses along our front fence; they grow and bloom well even under big shade trees. There were plenty of blackberry and sumac and wild rose thickets on each side of us, open woods on our back lot, pastureland across the road in front, and beautiful vistas of blue Ozark hills.

Birds loved our pokeberries, so abundant we talked about naming the place "Pokeweed Farm." One of the small canneries in our neighborhood offered to buy our crop of poke sprouts, to be canned as "poke salat," but they were all saved for the birds. We wouldn't think of cutting down the dead tree stumps on the place; all the woodpeckers native to the region, including redheads, the rather wary, big pileated and the uncommon hairy, liked our dead trees—and performed for our recorder. So did bluebirds, chickadees, titmice, and white-breasted nuthatches.

This was our first experience with rural living although we had both grown up in small towns during the horse-and-buggy era. Jerry bragged about having hoed corn "all summer long" (actually one day) when the weeds looked tall as trees and seemed as hard to fell. I distinctly remember having milked a cow—one pint of milk. Even as a child picking strawberries was my pet aversion. But visions of shortcake and jam, plus my Scotch heritage, which abhorred waste, compelled me to salvage the fruits in the nearly worn-out strawberry bed. It was a backbreaking job no matter what picking posture I tried. Wild blackberries were shared with the birds more freely because their price was one chigger bite for each berry—and the bites lasted longer.

It was a disappointment that there was no spring on our place, or a trickling stream, preferably one which would trickle soundlessly. Our tiny pond, a "tank" in Texas, did attract some birds, even an occasional kingfisher or killdeer. But it held a hazard for birds. Jerry happened to have his binoculars focused on a huge bullfrog on the bank one spring morning, when a yellow warbler flew down for a drink. The frog made a big leap and almost caught the warbler, which swerved just in time to escape.

There were many dogwoods in our woodlot, even a few with pale pink blossoms, also a few Juneberry, or shadbush trees. We found black haws, two kinds of huckleberry bushes, both of them low-growing, and a few real chinquapin trees. Most of the large white oaks, for which this region is famous, had been lumbered out of our woods when the house was built; the oak for our floors had probably grown on the place. A few patches of Mayapples, a clump of bracken, delicate wind anemones, and lovely crowfoot violets, as well as less showy species, grew in the woodlot. Yet we were not completely satisfied; there should have been wild red columbines with their yellow faces, pink Dutchman's breeches, yellow trout lilies, and sweet William phlox, all Ozark natives.

After spring rains there was a little temporary pool at the base of our wooded ravine and it was a magnet for migrating birds. A helpful friend even tried to dig it deeper, in the hope of developing a permanent seeping spring, but the rocky ground soon discouraged him. One morning I focused on a black-and-white warbler, just passing through. He has an extremely high-pitched voice and our recording was barely audible.

The densest "brambrew" brier was in Mout's pasture, next to us on the south. Since this was more than 500 feet from the house, Jerry had to carry an extra 500-foot reel of microphone wire through the fence and into an open spot in the pasture. Then I, having put the breakfast dishes in the sink, would start out, often wearing a leather jacket over my sweater, my slacks tucked into Jerry's outgrown rubber boots as we never found a way to prevent the heavy dews from soaking into leather boots. I really didn't have much to carry: just the thirty-inch reflector and tripod, a flashlight, a microphone, a folding camp stool, binoculars, sometimes even the Peterson and Saunders guides. But it was something to get everything through the rail-and-barbed-wire fence, in the dark, then stumble around in the pasture to find the extra reel, drag that line a few hundred feet to the edge of the thicket, then go back to connect the two lines.

Those birds were worth the early rising, the plodding through the dark, the chilly waiting! We never found it necessary to use a blind. If the listener is in place before dawn and doesn't move around much after, the birds are less shy than when approached in daylight. As Jerry put it, "If you can't act like a stump then act like a lazy, grazing cow!"

Yellow-breasted chats are usually retiring, but three of them seemed to be trying to chase each other from a favored perch, right in front of the reflector, one spring morning. It was the tallest sprout in the thicket. They went through all their clownish tricks, spouting straight upward like golden balls from a Roman candle, legs dangling loosely, wings flapping and clicking together over their heads. This clicking sound is faint but audible on our first LP record. Even when perched they were constantly jerking this way and that. The chat is listed as a daytime singer, yet, with one exception, the best

91

songs we have heard from chats were delivered shortly *before* dawn. The most outstanding song we ever heard from a chat, however, was given shortly after noon. Apparently it was an inspired courtship recital, an ecstatic performance lasting only a minute or so.

White-throated sparrows whistled softly under the rose bushes in Mout's pasture; white-crowns began as sweetly but ended wheezily. They eluded the microphone, but one morning two white-crowns ate grain at our doorstep. They came again the second winter, 1951–52, one an immature bird whose head stripes were still tan and brown instead of black and white. They sang for us the second spring.

Yellowthroats came so close, in the Mouts' wild rose-blackberry thicket, that I half expected them to take off their domino masks right in front of me. This was another place where we *almost* recorded a prairie warbler. For two summers, one in Kentucky and then the first season at Avian Echoes, we had been haunted by their weak, zizzy little voices, which leisurely climbed five shallow steps, tonally about quarter steps. It seemed to us that the prairie warblers in Florida, where we first met the species, had stronger voices than these. Not once had we seen the bird about our place, although the mysterious little voice came now from the treetops, sometimes from the sumac bushes back of the strawberry bed, often from the open pasture where we thought surely we could track him down and flush him.

Suddenly, one morning, there he was, right in front of the reflector, not ten feet away—and singing! I dared not move a finger, but was so excited and elated over this prize that I almost interrupted the bird to announce his identity. The prairie warbler caught at last! It was not until I got back to the house that I learned the bird voice had not come through. Possibly, in my excitement, I had failed to focus exactly on the bird. "Oh well," I sighed, "the prairie's is one of the less musical warbler songs, and most warblers are poor singers. Better luck next time!" The better luck came the next year, near Lexington, Virginia.

We even caught a Bell's vireo and a warbling vireo in the same tree on the same morning in Mout's pasture. It pays bird listers who are trying to list as many species as they can in one day to learn the songs of all the vireos, for these little, greenish, treetop birds are usually more readily distinguished by their songs than by their plumage.

"Pretty little nest here don't you think?" Bell's vireo says, saucily, often alternating with, "'f you don't get out of here you'd better!" Actually, he uses more notes than these syllables imply, but we could not translate the rest; he always goes too fast for us. The warbling vireo's notes flow together smoothly and more musically than the dry, staccato notes of the Bell's. Perhaps most difficult to distinguish of the more common vireo songs are those of the red-eyed and yellow-throated vireos, but once the hoarser voice of the latter becomes familiar the difference will nearly always be recognized. White-eyed vireos have the most varied songs: "Chip fell out of the white oak!" "Chip sisser weeah!" and many more, all delivered in a snappy style, and rarely could they be confused with any other species.

In the fall a redheaded woodpecker talked for us at our new Ozark home. This bird often displayed the personality of a garrulous bully and tease. Some bluebirds were nesting in an abandoned red-bellied woodpecker hole in a tree stump and the redhead made that stump his favorite drumming post—to the fluttering consternation of the bluebirds. Perhaps the woodpecker was jealous because he had failed in his own attempts to get his mate to nest in the same stump. One day we heard Mr. Redhead answering a tree frog with a very good imitation of the frog voice. It is said that these mischievous birds have a way of annoying hunters by following them

93

through the woods and keeping up a constant chatter. That winter we watched one immature bird as his head gradually changed from black to red.

Another bird we recorded during our first winter at Avian Echoes was a Lincoln sparrow. When we had discovered that his favorite singing perch was the topmost twig of a backyard brush pile, it was no trouble to record his whisper song. Part of the time he even perched on the microphone. Except for the lower volume, this whisper song seemed to be about like his full spring song.

John Kieran once wrote to us, "Why, some of your birds sing tunes that I had never heard before!" Bird songs are more varied and they vary in more ways than we had dreamed. We should have known this, for we had been listening to bird songs most of our lives and we had studied A. A. Saunders' indispensable *Guide to Bird Songs*. We began to realize that we should always be able to discover new tunes, even from the birds we thought we knew best.

"To be able to understand the language of birds is equivalent to being able to converse with the gods." The only person we know who understands the language of even one species of bird is Herbert Stoddard, who certainly has a very fair idea of what bobwhites are talking about. There are times when one has an inkling of what crows and jays are exclaiming about or whether a Carolina wren is expressing exuberance or scolding some intruder. We once met a man who claimed he could translate every single thing a blue jay says! Most of us are happy if we can even identify the voice of a bird without attempting to translate its meaning into human language.

We continued our interest in seeing how many different song patterns, or tunes, we could record from a given species. A book once described "the" song of "the" Carolina wren as "a clear, chanting whistle, a tri-syllable thrice repeated." Our collection of Carolina wren songs contained twenty-five different song patterns in some fifty recording sessions. The collection included about as many two-note and four-note phrases as it did of three-note, or three-syllable.

By autumn of 1952 we had twelve song patterns from white-eyed vireos and thought they were about all the birds could do. Then in late March of 1953, in the course of two mornings in the Big Thicket of East Texas, we got five song patterns we had never heard before from white-eyed vireos, in addition to some of the tunes we had previously recorded in other parts of the country.

About two months after we first began recording birds we had attempted to segregate and classify our cardinal songs, but gave up the job, temporarily, because the species seemed capable of almost infinite variations. Saunders relates that in three days, in Delaware, he noted twenty-eight different cardinal song patterns. We never did add the final score on our sixty-three recording sessions of this bird. This includes all subspecies recorded. Each of our twelve years of recording gave us new patterns from cardinals.

Despite all their variations the songs of a given bird species usually possess certain characteristics which make them recognizable. Consider three of the best-known bird songsters in America, all talented mimics: the mockingbird, the eastern brown thrasher, and the catbird. In spite of family resemblances, each species may be recognized simply because the mockingbird usually repeats each phrase several times in succession, the brown thrasher usually repeats each twice, or sometimes thrice while the catbird rarely gives the same phrase twice in succession. Any field sparrow may generally be identified by his song formula: two or three long notes, then a few short ones followed by a trill. Each individual of our five field sparrows at Avian Echoes could be recognized by his own variation of the species formula.

Years ago Schuyler Matthews published a birdsong guide,

now long out of print, in which he attempted to represent bird songs on the conventional, five-line, musical staff. It is an entertaining book, more distinguished for its literary merit than for its helpfulness. Renditions of such musical notations were once played on a piano for an ornithologist who knows bird songs very well. He was able to recognize only one species, the white-throated sparrow. But unless the piano player knew bird songs perhaps the test was hardly fair.

Then, in 1935, Aretas A. Saunders published his *Guide to Bird Songs,* using his now famous identification formulas and graphs, a sort of musical shorthand for bird songs. He used a combination of lines, curves, dashes, and curlicues, coupled with phonetic *syllabication.* The duration of a note was indicated by the length of a horizontal line, changes in pitch by relative vertical positions of the lines, glides by curved lines, trills by wavy lines, loudness by width of line. The tonal quality was described above and the phonetics given below each graph representing a song. His descriptive key is simple and carefully prepared. Each graph represents one specific song. After several of the more recent phonograph records of bird songs had been published someone suggested that Saunders' *Guide* was now superfluous. We can't agree. Might as well suggest that maps are superfluous if one has photographs!

The Saunders system did look a little difficult to understand, at first, but after some study we began to imitate it, in a crude way. Saunders states that an individual eastern meadowlark may possess a hundred different songs and he has over a thousand different ones in his notations. Although our best eastern meadowlark gave us less than fifty different songs we soon found that our musical memories could not be trusted to keep track of the variations; we *had* to use graphs. We also used our crude diagrams to classify songs of Carolina wrens, which are comparatively easy, cardinals, which are harder because of the glides and numerous variations, and of Bewick's wrens, which are so rapid, as well as high-pitched, that we found it possible to chart them only after reducing the speed of the tapes to one half or even one quarter. Bewicks have such varied songs that whenever I hear an unfamiliar bird song I am tempted to say, "Bewick's wren!" And we made diagrams of a few other species. It was another winter pastime.

Beginners should not be unduly discouraged by all this talk about variations in bird songs. There are many which are both simple and rarely varied: phoebes, which "say" their name while black-capped chickadees "sing" their "fee-bee" more deliberately as well as more musically; least flycatchers with their dry, incessant "chebeck"; bobwhites, simple most of the time; chipping sparrows. In a few cases the very simplicity of a song may be a handicap. Juncos and pine warblers, as well as chipping sparrows, have simple trills all on one pitch, or nearly so. But song characteristics which identify a bird are often easier to recognize than some of the obscure visual distinctions. And think how many times a bird may be heard but not seen!

It is not so surprising that individual birds of species with simple songs should sound almost exactly alike wherever heard, even holding to the same pitch all over the country. One phoebe, for example, sounds just like every other phoebe, ditto for the two songs of the nuthatch, for the downy woodpecker, the bobwhite, though he does have occasional odd calls, and for the chipping sparrow, although individuals do vary as to vocal quality. But we thought it was interesting that our recordings of a Dallas and a Fayetteville painted bunting are indistinguishable, to our ears; the same is true for two blue grosbeaks. These two species have fairly intricate and lengthy songs. On the other hand the orchard orioles we recorded in Texas, Kentucky, Arkansas, and Virginia showed

97

different but single song patterns for each individual bird. *Minor* variations do sometimes occur in one song pattern.

Two indigo buntings, which occupied adjacent territories at Avian Echoes, were easily recognized by the differences in their songs, even though each added notes and phrases as the season advanced. They were even recognized the second year when their territories had changed slightly. One of these buntings began the spring with "Pleased ta meetch-a"—no more. Later he added "no doubt" and finally a lot of rapid notes which our interpreter was unable to translate. One of our red-eyed towhees was especially hospitable; in addition to "Drink tea!" and "Drink your tea!" he also sang "Drink some more tea!" One titmouse had his own way of whistling "Here! *See* here!"

Eastern meadowlarks always had a strange preference for singing across the road from our recording setup. Microphone wire was too expensive to risk possible damage from passing vehicles. We solved the problem, to some degree, when we got our parabolic reflector. Our best recording was of a bird across the road from our Ozark home, about 125 feet from the reflector. He included one jerky little song, usually given in flight and so different from the rest that we had to watch long and carefully to make sure it was from this bird. But the funny little "Teedle-eddle, tee, tee" came from the meadowlark all right. Then we began to keep our ears open and sure enough—practically the same song is used by other meadowlarks in flight. Perhaps most eastern meadowlarks also include a "Laziness will kill you!" song pattern in their varied songs.

One trouble with using such word clues to teach bird songs is that the device is not always used with sufficient discrimination. Teachers have been known to fall into the rut of tradition. Because John Burroughs wrote that a white-throated sparrow sang "Old Sam Peabody, Peabody Peabody" does not prove that all whitethroats sing this song. In fact, out of hundreds of whitethroat songs, the nearest *we* ever heard that followed Burroughs' pattern was a *"Peeeee* body, body, body, body, body" that ran downward in pitch.

Many warblers have two most characteristic song patterns per species. Sometimes a black-throated green warbler sounds like "Trees, trees, murmuring trees" and other times like "See-me, see-me, see-me Suzy!" These are popular interpretations, but anyone who does not recognize which is which should resort to some other teaching device.

Another drawback to the word-clue method is that listeners' ears and imaginations are bound to vary. Even as some birds vary. A summer tanager, during two summers in the Dallas woods back of our house, varied his song only in the order in which he sang "Feature it! Genevieve, sweetheart, secret!" But we never heard another summer tanager with a song to fit those words. There was even some difference of opinion within the Stillwell family as to the value of such catch phrases.

Some of the more versatile singers include cardinals, mockingbirds, all the various thrashers, catbirds, meadowlarks, song sparrows, lark sparrows, Bewick's wrens, wood and hermit thrushes. Some tunes are used by many individuals of one species while others seem to belong to one individual. Saunders mentions that certain song patterns may be peculiar to a region, or even to a neighborhood. The two cardinals with peculiar cascade songs lived only about ten miles apart, near Dallas. Our Kentucky cardinal must have sung a regional song. A wood thrush sometimes has an individual phrase or style. An Avian Echoes larksparrow had a "Rio Rita" phrase which seemed to be his own.

It often seems that one pitch is prominent in the songs of several species singing in the same neighborhood, as if they tuned their pipes together. This made us curious. Using both the Saunders graphs and a list of the song-range frequencies published some years ago by Albert R. Brand, the Cornell pioneer of bird recording, we charted the song ranges of fifty-eight species of song birds. A few reach two or three half steps above the top note of the piano; three warblers and the grasshopper sparrow sing to more than an octave above the piano. Excepting the doves, owls, crows, and water birds, which were not included in the study, only about twenty of these songsters reach downward into the second octave below the top; only the Carolina wren reaches as low as the second octave above middle C, or approximately 1047 cycles (cps).

The highest note of a majority of the birds charted is between 4000 and 5000 cycles, or near the next to the top C of the piano. We looked for confirmation and found it in Saunders' *Bird Song*, published in 1929, a New York Museum handbook, page 73:

"When different species sing in hearing of each other, it is often noticeable that the pitches of certain prominent notes are identical."

And on page 74:

"In fact it is rather remarkable that a large number of songs I have recorded have the highest note pitched on C′ ′ ′ ′ ." This may help to explain why a technical expert with CBS, but not a bird student, expressed the opinion that, on our first record, "There seems to be a peak at around five thousand cycles." If true, it was because the birds put it there.

Rhythm (or time), pitch, volume, and pattern (or tune) may be shown by graphs. It is when we try to define differences in qualities of bird notes that language seems most inadequate. William Fish, who has done some outstanding bird recording in California, suggested that bird-song students should get together and evolve some standards of vocabulary in describing the songs. Dr. Charles Hartshorne, a professor of philosophy at the University of Texas, has recorded bird songs in many parts of the world and is engaged in a comparative analysis of the songs on a qualitative basis. We have used the word "reedy" to describe the quality of a blue grosbeak song and also for the somewhat different bluebird. We say that the cardinal's notes are "clearer" and "sweeter" than the Carolina wren's; yet some listeners do not agree to this, although they may confirm that the summer tanager's voice is "sweeter" than the robin's and that the scarlet tanager's is "hoarser." For greatest variations in tone qualities from one species, listen to a bluejay, or a chat, or to a lark bunting.

We learned never to say "never" about bird-song habits. We used to believe that hermit thrushes never sang in their winter territory; we often saw one in our wooded front yard in Dallas, in winter. Then once late in October, out at Camp Ellowi, the Camp Fire Girls' camp, another nature counselor and I heard one sing, only twice and far away, but we couldn't have been mistaken. We'd both heard our first hermit thrush songs at the Audubon Camp in Maine that summer. A leading ornithologist wrote that gray-cheeked thrushes do not sing during migration. Yet we heard them singing many times during their spring migrations through Dallas and Fort Worth. Maybe they like Texas better than the eastern states. Olive-backed thrushes migrate at the same time as the gray-cheeked and we found the differences in their songs quicker and easier means of identification than the color of their cheeks.

Our Ozark home was in the old Mount Comfort neighborhood, northwest of the university campus; a few of its buildings were visible from our windows. The neighbors were friendly folks and we enjoyed them, yet we felt like outsiders, perhaps more because we were not real farmers than because we were newcomers. One very lucky circumstance for us was that we already knew Dr. William J. Baerg, then head of the department of entomology and instructor in ornithology at the university, and author of *The Birds of Arkansas*. We had been schoolmates at the University of Kansas. Mrs. Baerg, Eloise, is a pillar of the cultural and religious circles of the town and campus, a charming hostess, and sympathetic toward birders. We met the interesting Laird Archers through the Baergs. They had spent several years in Greece while he was a technical advisor in agriculture. Evangeline Archer and I were kindred souls in our love of wild flowers and hatred of billboards. The Paul Rosses became friends through Jerry's need for expert technical assistance with his recording equipment. Mr. Ross is an electronics technician with the Civil Air Patrol and Mrs. Ross, though her first love is folklore, furnished much-needed appreciation, encouragement, and sympathy during our early days of hopes and disappointments when we were trying to find a publisher for our bird songs.

Two big fish nibbled our bait and then drifted away. Then we tried to sell some of our master tapes. In order to illustrate one possible use for the recordings, we prepared some sample discs whereon various bird songs were given as obbligatos to music we had recorded from radio. One of the samples was sent to the departmental head of a large radio network and when he finally returned the disc, which he had never unwrapped, his comment was illuminating. Condensing somewhat, he wrote:

"I just mailed to you the record which you sent to me, which I have not opened. In this business, when there is a price tag on a few bird notes, they just use any kind of bird, or none at all. After all, the use of the records is always in the background; secondly the quality of the records is very poor in every record I've heard to date. In order to get *good* bird effects, you would have to procure the services of a good engineer with modern, high quality tape equipment. So for a script demanding a particular bird, someone has to supply the necessary money, then we go out and make such a recording."

By this time we could have told *that* sound-effects director that it takes even more than a good engineer and a high-quality tape recorder to obtain a good recording of a wild bird song. We decided that radio director wouldn't have recognized our bird-song pearls even if he had opened the package. It is this attitude which causes them to use a mourning-dove song and call it a screech owl, or the screams of an eagle with a picture of a heron, and so on and on.

The Ficker publishers were found through an article about them in *Audio Magazine*. One reason we were anxious to find a publisher was that our increasing success with the recordings had increased our ambition to record songbirds over all of the United States. But we realized we would have to find a way to make our hobby begin to pay at least part of its own expenses. The number and variety of birds at Avian Echoes had justified our hopeful name for the place. They kept us busy recording every spring and early summer morning, when the weather permitted, through two springs. Now we wanted to visit new regions.

After the Fickers had indicated their definite interest in publishing a long-playing record of our bird songs, Jerry spent another month editing and splicing tape to prepare a twenty-minute sample of our best recordings. It was the following month, while we were waiting for their final decision, which was hardest to bear. It was clear to us why "the condemned man ate a hearty breakfast." His relief from the uncertainty was greater than his sorrow at his fate. Naturally, the Fickers wanted to consult an ornithological expert as to the quality and authenticity of our recordings. They went to Charles Mohr, then director of the Audubon Nature Center at Greenwich, Connecticut. He encouraged the use of word clues in the introductions to the bird songs on our record. He had found such clues very helpful in his teaching.

Fickers sent an enthusiastic "go ahead" on April 17, but it was May 12 when our copy received their final approval. I remembered how I had felt when John King said, in 1930, that he would use our "Woodland Notes" column in the Dallas *News*. When I left his office my feet did not seem to touch the sidewalk. I just floated down the street.

All during our first spring at Avian Echoes a flock of goldfinches reveled in the weed patch that had once been a vegetable garden. They sang and they flitted, matching their bounding flight to the rhythm of their "perchicorees." But they simply would *not* sing in one spot long enough for me to get the reflector aimed and Jerry to get the recorder tape rolling. A dozen or more of the birds had a frenzied singing festival through the first two weeks of June—and the wind blew the whole two weeks!

It was late June of our second summer when one of the blackcaps finally stayed on the highest twig of a brush pile long enough for us to record his sweet melodies. Then we remembered that goldfinches are late nesters and, naturally, would not begin to defend a fixed territory until long after other species were feeding their young. The goldfinch sang for us just barely in time to get on the record—and then he won the honored spot on the jacket! The record came out that September.

We began to breathe again, and sold the house trailer and traded the truck in on a new Ford station wagon. We had pulled the trailer more than 10,000 miles, left it resting in our backyard for two years, then sold it to a dealer in Tulsa— for less than half the first cost. We hadn't minded the crowded living quarters for a couple of years, but the worry of pulling it down the road and of finding good parking places was too much. As for economy, including the cost of the wreck and of alterations to the truck, it would have been cheaper to live at the best hotels. Moreover we wanted no trailer holding us back when we explored the mountains, east and west. Side trips had brought the truck mileage to over 30,000. It had served its purpose and it was a rattling success.

Chapter VII

YEAR OF THE HERMIT THRUSH[1]

Two important reasons why bird recording got off to a good start in 1953 were Pettingill's new book, *Guide to Bird Finding East of the Mississippi*, and a new, portable recorder, the Magnemite, weighing just twenty-five pounds and freeing us, at last, from the necessity of securing electrical power from farm homes. The machine was spring-wound and powered by small batteries. The converter, for which we had waited so long in 1950, had never been satisfactory and the manufacturer allowed us to return it. The new recorder was no toy; Dr. Kellogg had given the manufacturer considerable technical advice in its design, thus ensuring its suitability to the special needs of bird-song recorders. It arrived just three days before we started our season by a special trip to east Texas. It took most of the year, not so much to learn how to use the new machine as to develop our faith that it could do a good job. Therefore the Presto went along, too, and was still used whenever we could get current without too much trouble. The Magnemite had no immediate playback, no speaker, and no erase head, so we could not hear what was recorded until we got back from a day's trip; and all previously used tape had to be erased beforehand. The volume indicator was not as explicit as on the Presto, but the new recorder could produce

[1] The best of the successful recordings mentioned in this chapter appear on our second LP record.

high-quality bird songs, and, after 1953, we depended on it more and more on all our long trips.

On March 27 we started for Tyler, Texas, our equipment load now reduced to 800 pounds. The next evening our host and hostess, the B. B. Watsons, guides and mentors of Tyler bird watchers, invited some twenty of their friends over for a talkfest about birds. If it hadn't been an old story to the guests, the real center of interest would have been the Watsons' beautiful little backyard bird sanctuary. The Watsons even crack pecans and hang then from the clothesline so that the whitethroats and chickadees can get their share ahead of the squirrels and English sparrows.

Although oil-field traffic proved to be quite a handicap, we did manage to get a few good recordings in the Big Thicket region north of Beaumont, Texas, where we were guests of the Bruce Reids and Mrs. J. L. Hooks, who had cottages in the Thicket and were hobby naturalists, like us. Mrs. Reid included rehabilitation of injured birds among her nature hobbies while Mrs. Hooks was especially interested in native plants. Lumbering and oil developments have destroyed much of this once vast forest with its huge beeches and magnolias, longleaf pines and yellow poplars, and various oaks. There are many legends about early hunters and explorers being lost in its vast swamps. Today the Houston Outdoor Nature Club has set an excellent example by preserving a small segment of this unique forest. And a few individuals, like the Reids and Mrs. Hooks, were trying to preserve other segments of the region through private preserves, and by propaganda.

Dogwood, redbuds, and red-flowered buckeyes were just coming into bloom; small boys were already peddling buckets of Mayhaws, an early-blooming, large-fruited species of red haw, which is much prized for making jelly. We wondered why they did not add cypress knees to their wares; the knobs are often polished and sold as novelties.

As usual, more time was spent in exploring side roads, looking for good recording spots, than in actual recording. Breezes and showers took their usual toll. We often guessed wrong as to when and where the birds would sing. Yet three good recording mornings out of eleven days in the region was as good as average. Our best morning was at Pine Knot, Mrs. Hooks' cabin. We were awakened before dawn by a single, long, angry scream from some animal that we wanted to call a wild cat, but neighbors advised was probably a coon. Our first recording was of a hooded warbler, handsome in yellow and black, whose final phrase of "It's Greasy Sue!" had been haunting us for several days. Luckiest break of all was the ruby-crowned kinglet that chose a clump of low bushes in which to practice his whisper songs right in front of the cabin. He allowed me to bring the reflector within three feet! Except for the lower volume this song seems much like the one we recorded in the Tres Ritos region of northeastern New Mexico a few years later. Part of his song, though higher and much fainter, resembles one of the triple-note songs of a Carolina wren. This was enough to make a red-letter day, but we also got some good wood-thrush songs, although of course the chorus of wood thrushes Mrs. Hooks had hoped for was impossible. Our most versatile white-eyed vireo also performed for us this morning; In addition to the familiar tunes and some others new to us, he gave very good imitations of a bluejay and of a crested flycatcher.

It was after our recital at Beaumont, which we enjoyed very much because our listeners seemed to enjoy it, that we decided recording and recitals did not combine very well for us on the same trip, and thereupon canceled our engagements at Memphis, Louisville, Charleston, and one or two other places. The programs used up time and energy and held us to a fixed schedule. In spring nothing should interfere with recording. We kept our two dates in Dallas, one for the Camp Fire

Guardians and the other for the Dallas Garden Club. We felt very proud to be invited by that distinguished group.

Spring was tardy and fickle in 1953. We were caught in a "dogwood winter" at Otter Creek. The Johnsons welcomed us warmly and installed us beside a big fireplace at Van Buren Lodge, overlooking the river. A Louisiana water thrush teetered about the terrace but he didn't seem to like the sleet and snow any better than we did. No kind of weather for bird songs!

By the time we meandered eastward over Cumberland Gap, dogwood blossoms had again replaced snow flurries. At one cabin we were puzzled by the disappearance of several apples and two large bars of Ivory soap. Then we caught sight of a rat climbing through a broken window pane and carrying a bar of soap. Considering the advertised purity, the soap might be better food for us than some of the synthetics we consume without question.

Exploring side roads, we often ended at a mudhole where it was hard to turn around. But one day a side road led us to an orphanage where a casual conversation with one of the staff led to an impromptu recital of bird songs. The program was a failure because their old phonograph scratched and bucked, but we carried away a pleasant memory of a director who was making a success of his role as foster father to scores of boys and girls.

One good birder leads to another. We forget how we first met the Ben Coffeys of Memphis. He is a special student of chimney swifts. It was the Coffeys who told us about Mr. M. B. Cater of Clifton Forge, Virginia. His special interest is purple martins. Mr. Cater introduced us, by letter, to the Reverend Dr. J. J. Murray of Lexington, Virginia. The Murrays very generously lent us the use of their rustic cabin, a few miles from town and on the Maury River. Since Dr. Murray discovered the first cerulean warbler in Virginia, we thought it was especially appropriate when we recorded its song at his cabin. Here we also caught our best prairie warbler—at last—as well as a yellow-throated vireo, scarlet tanager, and redstart. We recorded fifteen species in our six days at the cabin, a good record for us.

Five days at Warm Springs and vicinity, in scenic Bath County, where the Bullpasture River flows through a valley with lush meadows and spreading shade trees, gave us a good score, too, with about twelve species new on our list. Best remembered at one plantation were some unquenchable house wrens, a flock of white-crowned sparrows, a yellow warbler, and the dawn song of an eastern kingbird. In the same vicinity least flycatchers were chebecking, but our most memorable catch was two vesper sparrows. We really earned those birds. We had to drag a thousand feet of mike lines up and down the steep hillside pastures and hop back and forth across the meadow brook while the vespers made up their minds where they wanted to sing for us. When we played back the recording that evening the sweet melodies made us forget our aching backs.

Mountain Lake, located on top of a 4000-foot mountain in southwestern Virginia, has an unusual history. Fifty years ago this lake did not exist. It is believed to have been formed after cattle had trampled mud into the outlet of a spring until it became blocked. Beautiful oaks, beech, pine, and hemlock climbed the steep ridge and surrounded the lake area. The winding road up the mountain leads only to a resort hotel and to the biological station where we were assigned a cabin. Since neither the hotel nor the station was yet in operation for the summer, we practically had the whole mountain to ourselves except for the caretaker at the station and a skeleton staff at the hotel. We arrived on May 14, when warbler migration was still in full flight. Many of the trees near our cabin were second growth, which brought the birds low enough for easy focusing. The branches were festooned with an invasion of measuring worms which no doubt inclined the warblers to linger with us. As Fisher remarked, in *Wild America:*

"Warblers, warblers everywhere, nor any time to think." He was near Asheville, North Carolina, on an April 13.

The chestnut-sided warbler was our most abundant species. It was as easy as picking plums to get both the "Wish-to-see-Miss-Beecher" song as well as their second choice, a more wavering upward flow without the emphatic "Beecher" ending. Our luckiest catch was a Blackburnian warbler, which sang from a branch just above our cabin porch; he sang just long enough for us to catch his song and then was gone and seen no more. His high, piercing flame of a song was appropriate from the flaming orange-and-black feathered mite. He joined our list of lucky once-in-a-lifetimes. Among other warblers recorded here were the high, thin notes of a Tennessee and of a black-and-white warbler. By a lucky aim we also recorded the high, lisping squeaks of cedar waxwings.

The most accommodating bird at the resort was a blue-headed vireo. He not only sang from the nest, about four feet high in a rhododendron bush, but allowed me to bring the reflector within twenty feet while he continued to give his full repertoire, including a less-common continuous warble. The blue-headed has the most musical of all the vireo songs. Two rose-breasted grosbeaks had established nesting sites on the campus and gave us the most beautiful songs of all the birds in this area. Their flowing melodies sounded like a robin that had received the training of a prima donna.

Our rarest bird view at Mountain Lake was of a pair of yellow-billed cuckoos holding their bills in a cross-scissors clasp while they were copulating. It required considerable neck twining. (We were reminded of Allan Cruickshank's famous photograph of a pair of kissing seals.) Even stranger was the mating behavior of a roadrunner, another member of the cuckoo family, which we later saw in the Saguaro National Monument near Tucson. The mounted male was pecking his mate in what appeared to be a most vicious manner. We thought, at first, that he was killing some smaller species. His courtship behavior is much like that of a turkey: strutting, tail-spreading, wings dragging, accompanied by queer, guttural sounds.

It was too early to see the rhododendron and mountain laurel in bloom at Mountain Lake, but lovely flame azaleas, in shades from yellow to deep orange and pink, were ablaze on the lower slopes. In the woods we found wild lilies of the valley and huge pink trilliums, four or five inches across. Carpets of bluets, dotted with the deeper hue of violets, reflected the sky. Tall, brown-fringed cinnamon ferns were unfurling in swampy spots.

One evening Mrs. Couch, the caretaker's wife, brought us two big chunks of cornbread, with fresh milk and home-churned butter. Our supper was a feast. The milk of human kindness again!

Eleven days without a single traffic interruption! We were sorry to leave this beautiful mountain retreat although the warblers were no longer quite as "thick as butterflies on a Gilliam honeysuckle bush," as I had written to Dallas friends.

At Durbin, West Virginia, we found a room in the postmaster's home. On account of our early rising habits we persuaded our landlady to let us cook our breakfasts in her basement, where we hoped we would be less likely to waken them. One morning I was hurrying but tiptoeing up the basement stairs with a few things to go into the kitchen refrigerator. Just as I got to the top step I glanced down to discover I had dripped grape juice all the way up! I mopped up as well as I could, but we are probably remembered to this day by the purple stains on those unpainted steps. The folks were polite about it.

Here we encountered a blackberry winter—on the twenty-sixth of May! No hermit thrushes could we find at Cheat Bridge or at Gaudineer Summit. Perhaps we were there too early in the season. One dawn we heard an extra musical song sparrow right on the main street of Durbin—and right beside the railroad track. A freight engine was puffing idly a few yards away. Jerry put on his most winning smile and persuaded the engineer to idle his engine several rods down the track. We caught the bird song.

Terra Alta was a very noisy place, with the Baltimore and Ohio trains puffing and screaming their way over the divide. A few miles back from the railroad line we found several interesting neighborhoods where we were able to record some of the birds we wanted. At the Oglesbay Nature Camp we recorded Baltimore orioles, song and swamp sparrows, and redwings, as well as others. At the Shays' cottage, in the same neighborhood, we got another Baltimore, after much patient waiting for him to give his full song, also more song sparrows, a veery, and a yellow warbler.

Bobolinks were our prize birds from the region. We caught them singing in no other. Our best chance to record them was at the Percy Teets farm, about twenty miles from Terra Alta. We found their favorite clover patch some distance from the house and got permission to use the electricity from a big barn nearby. It took three predawn trips over the narrow, roller-coaster road, once through a dense fog, before we taped their merry songs. Bobolinks are as fickle singers as goldfinches and have the same habit of singing in restless flocks. Three microphones were spaced along the meadow fence and I had to keep turning the reflector to pin down one or another of the singers until we had enough of their bubbling melodies. We never did hear one sing "Robert-of Lincoln," as implied by the poem I used to recite in the sixth grade. Even if I had been acquainted with their songs, in those days, I would not have been able to recite the words fast enough to give the right idea about the song.

One memorable Sunday the Ralph Hostetters, who had arranged permission for us to record at Mountain Lake, met us for a picnic lunch in the Terra Alta city park. Dr. Hostetter teaches biology at the Mennonite College in Harrisonburg, Virginia. A friendship begun by correspondence was climaxed by this meeting. He even liked our bird songs set to music. We were charmed by their gentle courtesy, shown as much to each other as to outsiders, and by a happy radiance in their faces.

Terra Alta remained our headquarters while we took several trips to beautiful Swallow Falls State Park in western Maryland. A dense grove of tall, dark hemlocks in the park was far enough from the waterfall so that we could record a wood thrush. He became our favorite singer of the species. Usually a wood thrush song is composed of several phrases, each one a little different from the preceding, sung in no particular order. One bird may sing six to ten different songs; each song lasts only two or three seconds and normally consists of three phrases. The first part is two low-pitched, low-volume notes, often inaudible except at very close distance and sometimes omitted; the second and principal part consists of two to five, but usually three, clear notes on different pitches, often making a singable little melody; the third part is a much fainter and usually much higher trill. The total range of many of the better bird singers covers about one and one-half octaves, that of the wood thrush about two octaves. The hermit thrush is considered by many to be the best bird songster of the eastern United States, but some people think the wood thrush is more pleasing. Perhaps one special charm of the hermit is his typical scenic New England background of tamarack, hemlock, and white birch.

On another trip to Swallow Falls we recorded a veery, leisurely twanging his uniformly down-curving phrases which seem to repeat his name. Many bird names represent their typical songs or calls: bobwhite, whippoorwill, chuck-will's-widow, phoebe, pewee, chickadee (calls or chatter), towhee, dickcissel, killdeer, bobolink, jay, grackle, curlew, chachalaca, willet, kiskadee flycatcher, among others.

Not far from the veery, two ovenbirds gave a duet from the floor of a wooded glen, each bird with a different accent in his two-note song. A black-throated green warbler gave his "murmuring trees" melody from a lower branch of a big oak. While we were trying to keep up with the capricious flittings and staccato melodies of a Canada warbler, we gradually became aware of a parked car some yards away and a couple of people who were very slowly and cautiously approaching us on foot. They were more careful than many not to disturb us while we were trying to record. We learned that the man was an electronics engineer serving on the Atomic Energy Commission. They eagerly bought one of our records and gave us some free advice. One bit we thought not very practical for our purse: he said our reflector should be silver-plated on the inside, because sound waves are reflected by the same laws as light. We had painted our aluminum black in order to make it less conspicuous to the birds.

One of the charms of the Cranesville Bog, near the line between West Virginia and Maryland, was its remoteness from traffic. One new bird for our files was a northern water thrush. We did not include him on our next published record because our taping of his logical partner, a Louisiana waterthrush, was not good enough. In a little grove of tall hemlocks, which we called "The Cathedral," we taped an antiphonal duet from a pair of black-capped chickadees. They are less versatile than our Carolina chickadees, but their tone quality is more pleasing because considerably lower-pitched. We also added some new varieties to our store of redwing calls.

The minute I saw Pocono Lake I had a happy premonition that *this* was the place! A few inquiries brought us to the home of Sterling and Alice Wagner. The most horrified look came over her face when we told her we wanted to get her hermit thrush. After we explained the "get" she and her busy forester husband cooperated in every way and we became the best of friends. Although she is quite a bit younger than we are, Mrs. Wagner has the typical attitude of a good graduate nurse: she mothered us, fed us, saw we had plenty of blankets for the cool nights; she fairly hovered over us.

Deep in the hemlock forest, that first evening, we found our chiming bird. Many New England poets and composers have been inspired by his ethereal chants. Do you remember "Sweet Evening Bells," "Sweet Sabbath Eve," "Juanita," "In the Gloaming," "Last Night the Nightingale Woke Me"? These oldtime songs express the mood produced by the hermit thrush. His spiritual equivalent is the European nightingale. I wondered if my father, who grew up in Pennsylvania and taught his children the old songs, had also loved the hermit thrush. At any rate, when our hermit thrush had finished his evening hymn there were tears in my voice as I announced for our tape record, "H–hermit th-thrush! Poconos L lake, June tenth." Jerry kept that announcement as a souvenir of our big moment. The next morning, in the same woodland lane, it was this bird that was so excited over his courtship, ignoring us, that he lighted for an instant on the rim of the reflector, inches from my face.

Near the lake shore our best recordings were of a flock of chattering barn swallows perched along a wire and of a Magnolia warbler. One song from this bird was so unusual that Saunders questioned it when he was asked to review our tape for LP number two that fall. We were very sure about the origin of the song, but if it was so untypical as *that*, it did not belong on the record and was cheerfully clipped out of the tape.

The old Old Greenwich Hotel, where we were guests of our record publishers, sits calmly on the bay shore like a retired capitalist who has no more pressing occupation than clipping the coupons of his gilt-edged securities. The place was so quiet we even recorded a few bird songs on the lawn back of the old frame structure. The Fickers entertained us most cordially, arranged a radio interview with Rhea King at Audubon House in New York, a television appearance in Boston, the latter sponsored by the Hyde Bird Feeder Company.

The Fickers urged us to get busy on another record. That was as funny as Jerry's Dallas boss once urging Jerry to get busy on some specification or program. If Jerry sometimes seemed slow it was only because he was so painstaking. Nobody in his life ever needed to urge Jerry to get busy about anything. He even kept the woodbox behind the kitchen range filled, without reminders, in the days when he wore knee pants. Dilly never dallied with Jerry.

June 19 ("June 'teenth"), Emancipation Day in the South, was a big day for us—we met two of the nation's leading bird watchers. One was J. Russel Mason, then a guiding spirit in the state of Massachusetts, which leads the nation in numbers and distinction of its bird-watching population. Just because Mason had mentioned the "habitational conferees" in his kind review of our first record, we were expecting at least a Harvard accent and a somewhat formal manner. We were happily disappointed on both counts. He wanted us to publish a record of New England birds only. Well, our volume II has a stronger New England accent than he himself has.

The other distinguished birder we met that day was Aretas A. Saunders. He and his sweet, adoring wife, his "Lady Grace," are both modest almost to the point of shyness. Yet her pride in his distinguished contributions to ornithology shines in her eyes. It's always fair weather when bird lovers get together and we thoroughly enjoyed our visit with them.

During two weeks in the Adirondacks one of the Valley View log cabins at Keene was our headquarters. It would have been our favorite region in the whole country for summer living, and we longed to see the hard maples in the fall. The light-green, lacy tamaracks of the bogs are always so symmetrical, tree perfectionists. Beech, hemlock, and spruce join the maples on higher ground. The lakes and mountains are scenic, but not awe-inspiring. Perhaps a sort of balance between human occupation and wilderness areas is one of the attractions. Lake Placid seems to deserve its name.

We enjoyed a scenic drive up Whiteface Mountain and a view, from its summit, of Lake Placid, as well as several other lakes. Both winter wrens and gray-cheeked thrushes sang along the mountain highway, but not in reach from the few, small parking turnouts.

Over at Ski Lodge, on a side road about halfway up the mountain, our luck was much better. One morning a fervent little purple finch sang his heart out from a tall, dying pine tree at one corner of the lodge. Usually such a phrase is not meant to be taken literally, but the next morning after our lucky recording session we found this tiny, raspberry-tinted fluff of feathers lying dead at the foot of the pine tree. There were no marks of violence.

On the other side of the clearing of the lower ski slope we heard a hermit thrush. Jerry got the car part-way down the slope and managed an electrical connection while I dragged a microphone line across the clearing. Halfway across I suddenly stopped. Jerry came over to see what was wrong. Nothing was wrong, but there in a little depression in the grass and ferns lay a spotted fawn, just as motionless as his mamma had told him to be. His big eyes looked worried, though. We retreated and chose a lower crossing for our line.

It turned out that only one singing site of the hermit's circuit was in reach of the reflector. Between recordings I had time to pick wild strawberries. Possibly this hermit was a better singer than the Pocono bird but a first love always holds a special place. We recorded an olive-backed thrush up there also.

Another hermit thrush, near the Mountain Lodge Hotel above Keene, gave us trouble because he was above a rushing mountain stream. Finally I found a trail by which I could get on the other side of the bird and point away from the brook. He was a good singer, too.

Our best olive-backed thrush song came from The Glen, a country settlement east of Keene. It took several trips to get it; sometimes there was a breeze, once the bird was not at home, once there seemed to be too many trees and bushes in the way. Thrushes seem to sing in the evening more than many other birds, but there are usually more man-made noises in the evening. However, it was one evening that we finally got the voice in The Glen. I had to scramble up a steep little slope, dodging underbrush and untangling lines and paraphernalia. The bird was especially wary, but fortunately the bushes were thick enough to conceal me. I had to find an opening for the reflector and brace the tripod and myself on the slope. The endearing song, which drops halfway back each time it makes a spiral curve up the scale, was preserved on our tape.

On our way home from The Glen one day we had a glimpse of the instinctive wisdom which guides a wild parent. A ruffed grouse was walking very sedately across the road a few yards in front of our car. She ignored our presence, no more to be hurried than a bride with eight bridesmaids. Then we discovered her reason as we saw eight baby grouse, no bigger than hazelnuts, skittering across in front of her, one at a time but each using wings as well as legs to scurry into the underbrush. When the parent bird was a bit more than halfway the last baby was safely across the road; then the older bird hurried after them.

In northern Minnesota, in the summer of 1957, we saw a duck, or similarly shaped water bird, with a different method of getting her offspring across the road. We were too far away to identify the species. What seemed at first to be a very thick and short snake squirming and weaving across the asphalt was presently resolved into a tight procession of birds, the head and neck of each follower resting on the back of the one in front of him. Just how they managed such a crouching gait we couldn't imagine.

Dr. Gordon Meade, director of the former Trudeau Sanitarium, especially for treating tuberculars and now closed for lack of patients, took us out to the Norton Fir Farm, where we secured permission to record in the wooded bog back of the house. The family dog was formally introduced so that he would let us in, around 3 A.M., without barks or bites. He all but offered to guide me to the birds. It was a fascinating spot, but required a lot of scrambling over fallen logs, both of my hands full of equipment, including the very necessary flashlight. I am more inclined to worry about snake bites than dog bites. We recorded some morning hymns from whitethroats, in the Norton bog, but the winter wren we especially wanted was not there, or not singing. In the nearby meadow we found an approachable savannah sparrow singing from a granite boulder. A meadowlark, in line with the savannah and our reflector, was just as loud, although 150 feet farther away.

Winter wrens don't always insist on a bog, but we have never seen one without at least one rotting log or upturned stump nearby. Perhaps because of frequent rains, or shallow soil, or both, a majority of the trees in this region are uprooted when they fall. We once saw an entire field fenced with these uprooted stumps laid side by side on edge, picturesque and efficient. One early frosty dawn we were celebrating the Fourth of July by trying for a winter wren in a bog near Bloomington. I hastily unreeled a few feet of microphone wire —this bog was too deep for wading—and carefully attached the microphone at the precise ten inches in front of the reflector. Jerry was unpacking and setting up the Magnemite as there was no electrical connection within miles. As he started to thread the machine a full reel slipped from his hands and two hundred feet of tape slithered to the ground in tangled spirals! The winter wren was singing his best while we recorders both struggled to untangle and rewind the tape. We were shivering in padded jackets, but had to take off our gloves. Our fingers got so stiff that we finally gathered up the whole mess, climbed into the car, started the engine and heater, and thawed our fingers. By the time the tape was rewound the wren had retired to the depth of the bog and both traffic and breezes were increasing.

We had to drive the thirty miles from our motel to the bog again in morning darkness, but the wren songs were worth it. The species has an exceptionally long song, eight or nine seconds of continuous notes, extremely high-pitched but musical. By copying the recording back and forth between our two-speed Presto and one of the other recorders, we were able to reduce the song to one-sixteenth speed, thus reducing the pitch four octaves. Then we were able to count about 165 notes in the song. What a speed record! As for his song pattern, the second half is practically a repetition of the first, except that the final trill slides down a little in pitch, as though the bird was running out of breath.

The Bloomington bog also gave us the loud, imperative "Quick! Three beers!" of an olive-sided flycatcher and the calls of a red-breasted nuthatch whose weak notes might be compared to a tiny tin horn or to the twanging of a rubber band.

There is an old resort hotel on top of Mount Mansfield, 5000 feet up in the Green Mountains of Vermont. It is famous among the bird fraternity as the summer home of a few gray-cheeked thrushes. Just as we had reluctantly learned to call them Bicknell's thrushes the AOU ordered us to go back to "gray-cheeked"; this time we complied willingly. By taking the ferry across Lake Champlain we had traveled from Keene, New York, to Stowe, Vermont, near the foot of Mount Mansfield, in a few hours. A conference with the resort manager gave us complimentary tickets up the mountain road. And, for once in our rambles, we might claim that our birds did "sing for our supper." The hotel manager invited us to play some of our bird recordings for the other guests, and when we checked out a few days later we found our bill cut in half.

The hotel is surrounded by stunted evergreens; the spot preferred by the gray-cheeks was just beside and below the parking area. Winter wrens and white-throated sparrows were also abundant and vocal in the area. The gray-cheeked song has a reedy quality somewhat like the veery's, but it is higher-pitched and more varied. I was a little disappointed in their songs—and imagined the birds at Gilliam's place in Dallas were better singers. Even adopted Texans get in the habit of thinking all things in Texas are either bigger or better. A myrtle warbler sang on the wooded knob above the Mansfield parking area.

At the Rutland bog, in southwestern Vermont, we caught our best swamp sparrow, a little goldfinch, alder flycatcher, and more song sparrows.

Near Summit, New York, elevation 2100 feet, we found a boggy pond edged with shrubbery but surrounded by meadowland. Here we recorded a bullfrog, an alder flycatcher, towhee, song sparrow, savannah sparrow, and a kingfisher, but not all of publishable quality. Then, at a bridge northeast of Worcester, we added another scarlet tanager, a chickadee, and an unidentified warbler.

On July 14 we stormed the ivy towers, repaying the Kelloggs' visit to Avian Echoes the previous spring. Our happiest experience was a launch trip and picnic supper on Lake Cayuga along with Dr. and Mrs. A. A. Allen, Mrs. E. L. Palmer, who is a distinguished paleontologist, and Mrs. Albert Brand, widow of the man who first started bird recording (at Cornell), and our hosts, the Kelloggs. The famous bird sanctuary and new laboratory was just being started that summer.

There was a good excuse for stopping again at Pocono Lake. We had discovered that much of our first hermit-thrush recording was marred by snaps, possibly caused by the several electric refrigerators in the Wagners' cabins near our woodland trail. We were able to record the same hermit thrush in the same spot and this time without any snaps.

Towhees and whitethroats were still singing in the Wagner wood lot across the road from their house. One morning Jerry got even with me for picking wild strawberries on the Whiteface ski slope. He parked the car right beside a tall blueberry bush loaded with the biggest blueberries we ever saw. Then he sent me to focus on a towhee heard singing down deep in the woods. I obediently pointed at the towhee, but caught onto Jerry's trick when I saw the blue stains on his fingers. I got back before the bush was stripped.

In a meadow near Wyalusing, Pennsylvania, a killdeer was flying erratically and calling, out of reach. Two barefoot country boys came by and, after learning our problem, offered to help herd the bird up our way. We saw no harm in trying. The boys were as skillful as sheep dogs and we taped the protesting cries of the killdeer.

Salamanca was headquarters for a few days while we explored Allegheny State Park in western Pennsylvania. More indigo bunting songs, alder flycatchers and more song sparrows. No wonder the last two words sound repetitious—we recorded song sparrows more than twenty-seven times on this

[9] A canyon wren sent his cascading melodies into Mitre Peak Canyon, between Fort Davis and Alpine, Texas. He sang first from the highest boulder, then came down to give his encore at forty feet.

[10] *Windsor Ranch, high above Pecos, New Mexico. Here we caught the song of a pine siskin without the usual goldfinch interference. Audubon's warblers and juncos were also recorded.*

[11] *Aspen and spruce near Tres Ritos, in the Carson National Forest of northeastern New Mexico. A ruby-crowned kinglet was our most co-operative bird here.*

[12] North of Walsenburg, Colorado, we recorded the black-backed variety of lesser goldfinch on one side of the lane, and the eastern species on the other side. Joey, on the calico pony, called them "wild canaries." The Spanish peaks are in the background.

one trip—and that counts only the ones worth saving. We ran the recorder on about as many more. They are especially difficult to record without some distortion. Altogether, we saved recordings on forty-one eastern and sixteen western song sparrows. We never tried to estimate the number of different song patterns. We discovered no difference between eastern and western song sparrows. Remember that, in the world of birds and trees and wild flowers, at least, the dividing line between east and west is neither the Mississippi River nor the Rockies, but the band of dry prairie and desert east of the Rockies, roughly the 100th meridian.

Avian Echoes looked glad to see us home on July 27, but we had to smoke the wasps out of the pump house before we could get the water started. It was good to forget about bird recording for two or three weeks while we showed the Ozark scenery to my sister and my niece and nephew who were entertained by swims in the creek, backyard baseball, and picnics in the woods.

When we got back to sorting and gloating over the treasures of our ten-thousand mile, four-month trip we found we had forty-one reels, fifteen minutes on each, of bird songs, including eight reels on hermit thrushes! To our own surprise we found we had captured all the most necessary species and enough variety to make the second LP record! All in one spring! Jerry's journal entry for October 17 notes that it took us three days just to review our twenty recordings of white-throated sparrows and select the ones to be used on the record. The completed tape was mailed to the Fickers on November 10. Another year of hard work and lots of pleasure. We never had more fun in our lives!

Chapter VIII

WE GO WEST

OUR desire to produce a record of western bird songs was
stimulated not only by a wish to complete a representative collection of bird songs of the United States, but also by
the fact that, in the west, we would be pioneering, for the
most part. Cornell had published one disc of western songs,
recorded by William Fish, presenting ten species of birds, and
had previously included about that many western birds on
their first record of "American Bird Songs." All were of excellent quality, but, obviously, there were not enough species
to really represent the west. We must confess to the very human desire to "get there fustest with the mostest." Our two
published records included several species not previously published by Cornell, but, on the whole, we had to depend on a
different method of presentation and arrangement and on
greater variety of song patterns to satisfy our publishers and
attract customers. Now we had the hope of a real "first."

Our bird-recording jaunts often seemed to get off to poor
starts—but they ended "happy ever after." When we left home
on February 15, 1954, the yellow narcissus had started to
bloom and elm flowers were almost open. By the time we
reached Hot Springs, Arkansas, only 150 miles south, red maples as well as elms were in bloom, weeping willows were leafing out, and a few golden forsythia bells were vying with the
flaming "apple blossoms" of flowering quince.

125

We ate lunch in the car, parked in a government trailer park. Several birds sang a few notes; one sounded like a swamp sparrow, but no swamp was near, and were those short trills from a junco or a pine warbler? We already regretted having left Saunders' *Guide to Bird Songs* at home, although it is for eastern birds and we were headed west. By the time we got our lunch off our laps the birds had wandered away.

The very first night out it turned cold again, so cold we found the blankets in our cabin too thin and lighted the gas heater. Then we stayed awake most of the night for fear we might be asphyxiated by that unvented heater. We got such an early start toward Little Rock next morning that we reached the city ahead of schedule. We explored the parks and residential streets until afternoon.

We were house guests of the Herbert Daniels; he was president of the Little Rock Ornithological Society, which had arranged a dinner in our honor. There we had the great pleasure of meeting Ruth Thomas, nature columnist of the Arkansas *Gazette* and author of *Crip, Come Home!* Later we gave a bird-song recital for a gathering of folks who expressed heartwarming appreciation. The program was repeated in Memphis the next night when we were guests of the Ben Coffeys. Their thanks were expressed in a most welcome copy of Pettingill's new *Guide to Bird Finding West of the Mississippi.*

The morning was warm again as we started south along the river. The rest of February was spent meandering back and forth along and across the Mississippi, humming "Old Man River," "Suzanna," and "Shrimp Boat" as we admired the huge magnolia trees, the live oaks dripping with Spanish moss, glowing masses of azaleas in rainbow colors around the old plantation mansions in Natchez, New Iberia, and points between.

At Audubon Memorial State Park, in Louisiana, we enjoyed the beautiful shade trees under which John James Audubon, in 1821, made some of his famous paintings when he lived for five months at the quaint Oakley Plantation. But the fox sparrows which we hoped to find tuning their pipes around there, before we headed west, tuned not for us. Our motel cabin in picturesque St. Francisville, near the Audubon Park, left something to be desired. That night the mice held a party in our wastebaskets and the hole in the floor was so big we were relieved that the mice were not joined by larger varmints.

In various roadside mud puddles both colored and white folks were plying long-handled dip nets, about a foot in diameter. We learned they were after crawdads (crayfish), some used for fish bait, the tails of the larger ones going into the skillet. Jerry tried them at one country restaurant, said they were "fair, a little like shrimp."

Pine cutting was still a big industry in the region around Biloxi and New Iberia, and some turpentine was collected. Huge stacks of pulpwood were corded along the railroads. But many young tung orchards told of a newer industry. Down in the delta, citrus groves filled the landscape, except close to New Orleans, where truck gardens took over.

I celebrated my February birthday by the discovery of a new talent: I talked my husband out of jail! The trouble started with a misunderstanding of motives when an imperative traffic policeman in Chalmette whistled Jerry down for driving at twenty miles through a fifteen-mile school zone. It was early and children had not yet started to school. Jerry thought he was the victim of a speed trap and "sassed the cop." To complicate matters, I had to stop at a filling station after the policeman had ordered, "Follow me!" It took some honking and talk to persuade the officer, who understood French better than English, that we were not trying to sneak away or defy him. At the police station Jerry was taken to the jail, his billfold, keys, and belt taken away from him! I was told I was "free." It was too early to find many officials in their offices. But after many inquiries I found a "judge" to listen while I inquired, half laughing but worrying, "How do I go about it to get my husband out of jail?" It all ended happily with Jerry and the policeman shaking hands. The understanding judge in the court advised him, "Always agree with a police officer, even if he says that black is white."

Avery Island was rather a disappointment. Redbud and dogwood were in bloom, but we had arrived at the wrong season. Practically all of the famous snowy egret colony was gone. We admired the gardens and arranged with the owners to visit their nearby farm—the overseer would be directed to leave the key to the farm gate where we could find it early in the morning. But the overseer forgot to leave the key and by the time we got into the farmyard ditch-digging machines and other sounds of industry were beginning. Our only catch was some calls from a few Canada geese which may have been tame instead of the wild ones—not that we ever heard of any difference in their calls, but we had sentimental notions against recording birds tamed or in captivity. They were contrary to the unwritten rules of our game.

Myrtle warblers winter in this region by the thousands. Their soft *chit* was heard everywhere we stopped, town or country. But not a note of song! We heard two white-eyed vireos in a cypress swamp near Chacahoula, also one pine-woods sparrow, one swamp sparrow, and one unknown. Yaupon berries on Cypremont Point attracted a flock of a dozen myrtle warblers. Rattan, swamp privet, and an especially thorny greenbrier all held berries for the birds. Palmettos, iris, and calamus lifted their green daggers round about. A few fields of young cane shoots followed the swordlike pattern.

At a roadside park near Sulphur, Louisiana, we heard some gossip from a man who was moving a small load of household goods in an open-top trailer:

"I'll give you the setup on these game preserves. The land

is owned by a big lumber company. I've been in the lumber business for years. After they cut the timber they lease the land to the state for a game preserve, so they won't have to pay taxes on it. And so that is the setup. There's a rabbit every four hundred miles. My son-in-law is now in the pea-patch [jail] because he took a shot at one of them deer in off season."

From Lake Charles we took a round trip through the Sabine National Wildlife Refuge, crossing on about a dozen ferries during the course of the day. Much of the area consists of grassy marshlands, with wild rice edging some of the canals. At one place we were in sight of a beach and stopped to go over and look around for wading birds. We had walked only a few yards when we were surrounded by such a horde of hungry mosquitoes as we have never encountered before or since. As we dashed back to the car I had to shut my mouth, use one hand to screen my nose, while brushing the pests away from my eyes with the other. Even a bird song could not have kept us! I spent the next fifteen minutes swatting the blood suckers that had gotten into the truck. Mosquito Hollow, in the Ozarks, was never as bad as this.

A few blue and Canada geese lingered in some of the meadows. Boat-tailed grackles and redwings were abundant. A few shore birds and large waders, as well as herring and laughing gulls, were seen along the bayous and canals.

Down on the Gulf Coast, east of the refuge, in Cameron Parish, the village of Grand Cheniers is one house wide and several miles long, following the low ridge of live oaks between the gulf and the marshes. This is the region where, a few years ago, a hurricane wiped out so many of the homes, and some of the people. Almost none of the survivors moved away. They promptly set out to rebuild their damaged or destroyed homes.

From Orange to Galveston our road followed along the shore; we saw flocks of snow and Canada geese, few shore birds; the water was rough, wind high and cold; spring was having another of her relapses. March blew, as usual. Much wind, but there was not one drop of rain on us from March 5, the day we reached Harlingen, to June 15 in western Kansas, on our way home from our big circle in the southwest.

Down in the Valley we had good company to speed the windy days—the Gills, the Luther Goldmans, and Anna May Davis. Irby Davis was off recording Mexican birds, as usual. We slept at a tourist court this trip, but ate many dinners at the Gills.

At Atascosa Refuge we thought we were sneaking up on a few sandhill cranes, but, when the reflector and my eyes peeked above the top of the sand dune, the cranes had quietly sneaked out on us. We did record a few Cassin's sparrows and Bewick's wren songs, and a distant pauraque duet, accompanied by nearby frogs. We tried for a roadrunner, which sat on a creosote bush pushing out some strange moans that sounded as forced as they looked.

At Santa Ana Refuge the various doves were our despair. We needed a larger reflector for their low pitches. This was the year we recorded the conversation between a Derby flycatcher and a Harris' hawk, and the clacks, chuckles, squeals, wolf whistles, and creaking wheels from a boat-tailed grackle.

West Texas was dry. At Sanderson they had not had more than a sprinkle in the last eight years! We saw only one scrawny, wilted, hand-watered tree in the whole town. Big Bend National Park, in normally dry country, was better able to survive the drouth. The slender canes of ocotillos were almost leafless, their way of conserving moisture, yet their tips were flaming with blossoms. Down near headquarters trees began to appear; there is a weeping juniper which is unique to this region; Douglas fir, ponderosa pine, Arizona cypress, and western maples here find their eastern limits. A few birds were seen at Hot Springs, at the mouth of Tornillo Creek on the Rio Grande, the flaming red and black of vermilion fly-catchers and the yellow-patched gray of an Audubon warbler, the most notable. Feeling that better prospects were ahead, we returned to the main highway and spent the night in a delightful kitchenette apartment at the Highland Motel in Alpine.

During a four-day stay at Fort Davis, in west Texas, we got our first house-finch songs. In many parts of the west these pleasing singers, like house sparrows tinted with a shade usually raspberry but occasionally orange, are almost as common as house sparrows in the east. In California they are often called "linnets." We also got our first brown-towhee songs here.

The bright star of this region was a canyon wren. We had gone over to the Mitre Peak Girl Scout camp in a little wooded canyon walled by huge boulders, about halfway between Alpine and Fort Davis. The camp takes its name from a steep-sided, triangular mound facing the canyon mouth. At first the bird sent his silvery notes cascading down from the top of the canyon rim 200 feet or more above us. We eagerly recorded every note. Then the obliging mite came down to a boulder only forty feet away and repeated his entire concert! What a beautiful singer! He had about three styles of delivering his descending scales but the differences were not great. It is the sweet, ringing quality that makes the songs so breathtaking. We voted him the best singer in his family, even more beautiful than the Bewick's wren, which does have more variety. He easily rates among the best ten singers on our western record of sixty-eight species.

Heading west from Fort Davis, early in the morning of April 1, we counted eighteen jack rabbits and two small herds of antelope in the first twenty miles. Jerry remarked on how much smoother, as well as faster, is the gait of an antelope than that of a deer. We timed a raven at forty miles an hour as he flew for a mile straight down the road in front of our car.

Near the village of Patagonia, Arizona, close to the Mexican border, we came on a beautiful natural park, reached the shade of tall cottonwoods by fording a sparkling stream, Sonoita Creek. Here were ash trees, willows, and sycamores, little tree elderberries and tree tobacco, a welcome oasis after many miles of dry desert. There seemed to be a migration wave, birds, as well as dude-ranch visitors, heading north. The beautiful painted redstart was added to our life list although we did not get to record it until later. The birds included such colorful beauties as vermilion flycatchers, Bullock's orioles, Audubon's and Wilson's warblers, and purple finches.

To Erle Morton go thanks for much of our good luck around Tucson. He showed us his favorite birding haunts, introducing us to Indians on the reservation and to the owner of Agua Caliente Ranch. Mr. Morton is a retired mining engineer who takes beautiful color slides of birds with the aid of stroboscopic lights. The Mortons' walled garden, canopied by two bottle-brush trees fringed with red blossoms, is a bird sanctuary. Here we recorded close-ups of cactus wrens, Inca doves, Gambel's quail, and Gambel's white-crowned sparrows. The tune used by the latter sounded exactly like one of those we had recorded back in Bath County, Virginia.

The palm-lined driveway of Agua Caliente Ranch, near Tucson, was the frolicking ground for several hooded orioles whose sweet but weak voices were hard to capture, especially as the birds were so frisky and capricious. Fortunately for us, the palm trees were not very tall. Slurred notes, rapid warbles, and dry, chattering notes followed no order or time schedule. It kept me guessing as to which of the half-dozen birds frisking along the driveway would sing next. Whenever I caught a good focus quickly enough, Jerry turned the Presto lever to "record" and a few seconds of hooded oriole notes would be ours. As this species not only has a weaker voice but sings less frequently than other orioles, this was a lucky day. Movie photographers should have been there for some of the oriole wrestling matches.

Jerry inadvertently cut off a lesser (green-backed) goldfinch just as he stopped singing like a solitary vireo and began to sing like a goldfinch. One bird man questioned this vireolike song on our record but we were sure—and this type song is described for the species by Hoffman in his *Guide to the Birds of the Pacific States*.

Three large duck ponds were big attractions for birds at the ranch, the northern pond also serving as a reflecting basin for the Santa Catalina mountain range. An extra-versatile brown towhee must have studied under an Arizona cardinal; his favorite singing perch was in a hugh mesquite which threw lacy shadows over the blue-tiled swimming pool. Irby Davis later confirmed our recording of a beardless flycatcher, a nondescript little gray bird with a very high, whiney voice. Lucy's warblers, Inca doves, coots, a kingfisher, and other species were also taped at Agua Caliente.

There were no surfaced roads into the Indian reservation and the hazards varied from clouds of dust to slippery mudholes where irrigation water had overflowed into the roads. But traffic was light and the bird life varied. Some of our best vermillion flycatcher, verdin, pyrrhuloxia, and western kingbird songs came from the reservation.

At the foot of the Santa Catalina Mountains, north of Tucson, Sabino Canyon carries a clear stream edged with sycamores. Beyond the banks saguaros and other cacti take over. It was necessary to find our singing birds back some yards from the stream and to be able to point the reflector away from its babbles. Here we had to use the Magnemite recorder. Just as we had parked and started to unload equipment, a slim, grayish-brown bird with a faintly streaked breast and a down-curved bill perched on a waist-high boulder only a few feet away and began to sing. I kept behind the car until I had the microphone, reflector, and wire to the recorder all ready and then advanced slowly but steadily toward the singer. He not only let me come within fifteen feet of his rocky perch but faced me and defiantly continued his song! A curve-billed (Palmer's) thrasher song was captured on our magnetic tape. He was so close we could see the wild expression in his orange eye. The sharp "whit-wheet" call note, so distinctive of the species, was also recorded.

Saguaro National Monument, a tract of desert hills on which the treelike saguaro cactus is abundant, gave us an excellent place to record the full vocabulary of Gambel's quail. They were fed each morning just outside the museum's picture window. Dawn songs of Say's phoebe and ash-throated flycatcher were taped in the same area.

Eight days at Mesa, near Phoenix, went by like antelope. One reason was the Arizona Stillwell cousins whom we hadn't seen for years, and found very congenial. Jerry's nephew, then a senior in high school, was very interested in sound recording and the two talked shop 'way over the heads of the rest of us.

In the region around Mesa western meadowlarks were the prima donnas, though not temperamental. Their voices are loud and clear, lower in pitch than the eastern species, and most of their varied tunes are in major keys. We *think* we recorded forty-two different song patterns from them, on this entire trip. They were cooperative about returning to a roadside singing perch after we were set up.

One of our favorite recording sites, near Mesa, was the Coon Bluff Picnic Grounds; the place was deserted except on weekends. The clear Salt River flowed swiftly but quietly along one side, and the bluff on the other side sheltered us from traffic noises and breezes. The dawn song of an ash-throated flycatcher and a bit of the Arizona cardinal used on our western record came from here. Bendire's thrasher, with a continuous warble, in contrast to the separated phrases of the curve-billed, was recorded in the brushland near Mesa. Also from the Mesa region were a dawn song from a western kingbird, and, we believe, the *only* song of Bullock's oriole—he seems to be the least versatile of his family.

Gale Monson, author of the Arizona chapter of Pettingill's *Guide*, kindly confirmed our recording of a rock wren at Parker Dam. This bird was unusual because part of the time he sounded like a house wren.

Banning, California, was one of our best recording regions, thanks largely to Belle Wilson, who is remembered in Dallas as such a keen bird observer. It was she who had first discovered the black-chinned hummingbirds at Dallas. In Banning she was official field reporter for *Audubon Field Notes* magazine. We recorded fifteen species in five days! Fisherman's Retreat, a few miles southwest of Banning, had a grove of live oaks as well as a small lake between prairie foothills. Here we recorded our first yellow-headed blackbirds, most unmusical of the family, and, by great luck, our only Lawrence's goldfinch. At first I thought I was pointing at a house finch, so numerous around there. The singer was on a rather high, horizontal branch of a live oak, perched beside a nest! When the binoculars were finally focused and showed the black face and gray body, with yellow on breast and wings, I was so excited I interrupted the singer, one of my foibles, to announce his name. We saw this species around Mesa and elsewhere, but never again under recording conditions. Tri-colored blackbirds, several song sparrows, and more house finches were recorded by the lakelet.

Driving south from Banning one April morning, we reached the chaparral-covered foothills where human habitations were delightfully rare. The road had retrogressed from blacktop to sand in the valley, to natural rock and gravel on the slopes.

Parked on a shelflike turnout of a steep slope, we heard a bird reminding us of the sweet, clear songs of field sparrows. But the opening note was too high and too faint; besides, field sparrows belong east of the Rockies. Searching the slopes with binoculars, we finally discovered two of the singers, gray-headed, black-chinned sparrows, the first time we had ever heard their songs.

I scrambled for the reflector and attachments in the back of the station wagon.

"But Jamie,[1] those birds are too far away. We couldn't possibly record them!" Jerry was often the pessimist at this stage of the game.

"But maybe one will come closer. Come on Jerry. Remember the Balmorrhea owl!" I was reminding him of our most tragic experience in "he who hesitates is lost." In west Texas a horned owl had called from a little patch of trees, near Balmorrhea, only a few feet from us—and in broad daylight! We were so sure that such a phenomenon could not last that we stood there, motionless, and missed the best chance we ever had to get a *good* horned-owl recording.

Jerry pulled the Magnemite from its place behind the driver's seat, and unpacked it with an air of magnaminously indulging a feminine foible. One of the black-chins did come closer, and my focus was lucky. This was the only time during our three springs of recording in the west that we even heard the song of a black-chinned sparrow. It was not until the playback, later, that we noticed the wren-tit singing in the background.

Our first black-headed grosbeak, first western house wren, and first spotted towhee were recorded in International Park, north of Banning. The western house wren is more versatile

[1] Nickname for all Jamiesons.

136

than the eastern, but the towhee, now to be called rufous-sided, same as the eastern bird, gave us only a weak, buzzy "speeee." Our strongest objection to the official changes in the common names of birds, as published in the fifth edition of the American Ornithologists' Union's *Check-List of North American Birds*, is against giving the eastern and western towhees the same common name. They don't look alike and they don't sound alike!

The maze of expressways through Los Angeles to Hollywood was braved, not to gaze at movie stars, but to celebrate the May Day birthday of Jerry's sister Rena. In spite of our early hours, she went with us on several of our recording jaunts.

Although Griffith Park is fairly close to the business district, it is so large that, with the help of its wooded hills, we actually had more recording success there than at the Audubon Society's San Gabriel Wildlife Sanctuary at El Monte, where we were greatly handicapped by the roar of trucks, or the Tucker Sanctuary, near Santa Ana, where the bubbling brook was often a hindrance. Griffith Park gave us our only good wren-tit. This state bird has a loud voice—we sometimes hear it in motion pictures and television—but he is very secretive and therefore hard to get in focus. His notes are all on the same pitch, becoming faster and louder. One part of the five-square-mile park consists of hills covered with dense brush, still in a natural state except for the road. I tried again and again to get the bird in focus before Jerry finally said, "Hold it!" As was often the case, I had been in too much of a hurry to take time to mount the reflector on its tripod; my hands were full, holding the reflector in position, so I was unable to use the binoculars until the recording was finished. In this case it didn't matter, for the bird refused to show his white eye and angled tail until after the recording was completed.

The valley of the Tucker Sanctuary was widely known as

Modjesca Canyon, after the famous singer who once had a country home there. The sanctuary was given to the California Audubon Society by Mr. B. F. Tucker in memory of his wife. It is especially famous for the hordes of hummingbirds which are fed from test tubes lined along the porch of the head-quarters cottage. I had the assistance of young Dr. James Lane, then the sanctuary director; he not only named the new bird songs but helped me drag microphone lines from one song perch to another. We recorded a little valley quail, spotted towhee, canyon towhee, and plain titmouse. This tit has a weaker voice but a larger vocabulary than our eastern tufted titmouse.

At the San Gabriel Sanctuary we met young Sandy Sprunt, on his way to serve as a bird instructor at the Audubon Camp at Truckee, California. We told him our troubles about find-ing cooperative black-throated sparrows. He said they had been plentiful and singing at Palm Springs just a few days before. So we backtracked about two-hundred miles and recorded the one and only black-throated sparrow we found anywhere around there.

Oak Glen, east of Redlands and northwest of Banning, pro-duced a mountain quail and both Steller's and California scrub jays. The steep hillsides have apple orchards on the lower slopes, pines and live oaks on the upper.

Beautiful Mill Creek Canyon is near Oak Glen; the nearest town is Yucaipa. This scenic valley gave us the songs of twelve species of birds in just three days, despite the roaring stream. Dr. John Goodman, of the Redlands University faculty, was our guide and teacher in the canyon and he produced almost every bird we had hoped for except the elusive solitaire. Moun-tain chickadees were our favorites here; their songs are more varied than the two-note tune of the eastern black-capped. One here sang "three blind mice"; others had as many as five notes, the pitch usually descending. Some of our partiality had its beginning years ago when such mountain mites ate chopped peanuts from our hands, on Mount Wilson. We tried to remember the little verse:

With a fairy touch and a quick, bright look at me
A chickadee has lighted on my hand!

"How can I get a wild bird to eat out of my hand?" a child sometimes asks. We can't be very helpful as it requires longer patience than we could give, but we sympathize with the desire. It seems to require even more patience than recording their songs.

Our cabin in Mill Creek Canyon was above 6000 feet. Up the canyon a short distance, at 6300 feet, the remains of a winter snowdrift made roads too slick for driving. Incense cedars grew 100 feet tall. Western wood pewees, black-headed grosbeaks, long-tailed chats, western tanagers, and a western variety of the solitary vireo were taped.

Big Bear Lake, in the San Bernadino Mountains, at 6750 feet, is seven miles long and surrounded by tall pines and incense cedars except at the shallow upper end, which drains a meadow. The lake is an extremely popular fishing resort, but most of the cabins were not yet occupied in mid-May, a fact which contributed to our good luck with our kind of fishing. There were many passable side roads in the region and we explored all of them.

Our best singer at Big Bear was a slaty-headed, rusty-tailed, western fox sparrow, discovered at Pine Knot Picnic Ground, not far from our cabin. We had unloaded our equipment and made all connections before a bird was heard. Then the accommodating fellow came over and sang from a low branch in plain sight. He was easily identified, offered no recording problems, and gave a good variety of song patterns. He is not as pretty as the eastern bird, but an even better singer. Such glides and trills! He was another of our top ten of the best western songbirds. Perhaps the reason I failed to shed tears of joy over this first fox sparrow was that we found him before I had worked up that hope-long-deferred feeling that greeted our first hermit thrush.

Green-tailed towhees sang songs similar to the fox sparrows', a little thinner in quality and without as many glides. One which we recorded at the Gauke Ranch, about seven miles south of the lake, at 7500-foot elevation, surprised us by including a catbird-like "meow." Our pygmy nuthatch was found on this ranch.

Up at Sugarloaf settlement Mrs. Kountze fed the birds in her dooryard. Here we caught acorn woodpeckers, a few notes of a white-headed woodpecker, more Audubon warblers, and both Cassin's and California purple finches. An Oregon junco and a good duet of mountain chickadees were taped near her cottage.

One of the western bird songs we had our hearts set on, and never caught, was Townsend's solitaire. They nest in the region, but we did not even glimpse one. Brewer's sparrows ran their toy sewing machines in the marsh grass at the upper end of the lake, but we couldn't get the salt on their tails.

As we were leaving the Big Bear Lake country, after a happy week, coming down from the mountain through a steep, rocky gorge (the northern exit) we met an extra-versatile and co-operative rock wren. The species is as dry-voiced as his habitat is dry, sounds something like a Carolina wren who might have sung so much he'd almost lost his voice, like a politician on the last day of his campaign. He is about the size of the Carolina but grayer, as if the dry climate had made his feathers fade. But all of the wren family are lively, full of pep and personality. This bird gave us six different song patterns!

When we got down into the Mohave Desert we kept a sharp lookout for Scott's orioles. Their color pattern is similar to the Baltimore's, but they are yellow where the eastern birds are orange. Their voices are almost as rich and full as the Baltimore's and their songs are longer and more varied. It was one of our most-wanted western species and we had not yet seen even one. Finally, at the edge of the town of Apple Valley, we saw the bird, perched on a tall yucca, as was to be expected. Before we got near, the bird took flight. We chased him block after block, to the edge of the town, but he got away from us. He was the only one of his kind we saw this whole season.

Sequoia and General Grant national parks scarcely made us pause. The trees were just too tall for bird recording. The only two we recorded we couldn't see well enough to identify.

Yosemite was a disappointment. We couldn't get away from the roaring waterfalls and the noisy tourists. Up along the Glacier Point Road, where snow patches still lingered in late May, we did get some McGillivray's warbler songs (he likes bushes close to water) and more recordings of fox sparrows.

We had intended to start eastward through famous, shiveringly remembered, Tioga Pass when we left Yosemite, but the snowdrifts had not yet been cleared away. State highway number 49, named in honor of the "forty-niners," goes north through the center of the state. It was interesting, historically, huge tailings of gravel were still visible along the streams, and cabins in Sonora, Sutter Creek, and Placerville carried signs telling of their part in the romantic Gold Rush days. Steep meadows with scattered blue oaks and scanty-needled Digger pines made unique landscapes, but I found the bare drop-offs, combined with hairpin turns on the one-car-wide, two-way trafficked highway, detrimental to the enjoyment of scenery. If birds had sung I insist I would have heard them, though.

Lake Tahoe, even deeper blue than memory had painted, with snowy peaks scalloped above the western shore, offered few bird songs and few side roads where we could get away from traffic—only three species recorded in two days. Here, at the turning point of our trip, increasing winds began to hasten our homeward travel. In this area, and through all high-mountain forests and wooded canyons, we began to be haunted by our mystery vireo, variously announced on the tapes as "species unknown," "that little gray bird," "looks like a warbling vireo," or "tit-willow." One in Cimarron Canyon, in northern New Mexico, continued to sing from its nest; we could have reached out and touched it, but that would have been ungrateful when he had already tried to tell us his name. The habitats did not fit the gray vireo and the songs were not like the solitary vireo we had recorded at Mill Creek. The solitary sounded like its eastern counterpart, the blue-headed. We wished someone as competent as Saunders had published a guide to western bird songs. It took much reviewing of our records and the advice of some experts to persuade us that these were western warbling vireos. It seemed to me that the songs were much more broken by pauses than are those of the eastern variety.

No recordings were possible at Zion National Park—too windy—and our only souvenir of the majestic and inspiring Kaibab Forest on the north rim of Grand Canyon was a few phrases from a rather distant hermit thrush. His song was an exalted expression of the spirit of the place. We admired the handsome black squirrels with the white tails, found only in this region.

Scenic Pecos Canyon, northeast of Santa Fe, was full of fishermen and the roar of the river. A side road took us up to the Windsor Ranch, elevation 8640 feet, where it was very quiet. Our cabin held five beds and both heating and cooking were provided for by a massive, wood-burning range with six top lids for pots and skillets. We continued to cook on our lit-tle electric hotplate. Jerry found the ax and chopped up enough aspen wood to relieve the morning and evening chill.

There were enough cracks between the logs of the cabin walls to satisfy the most rabid fresh-air fiend. The sink was directly under a cupboard of such proportions that bumped foreheads were inevitable.

The greatest asset of the Windsor Ranch was a lonely auto trail, its narrow track wandering between groves of pine and aspen with vistas between of snow-capped peaks. Birds were rather scarce, but we found Audubon's warblers and juncos. The real prize was a pine siskin frisking his yellow patches in a low thicket beside a seeping spring. We were thankful that he had, for the moment at least, forsaken his usual gold-finch companions because many of his notes are so similiar that we might have had trouble distinguishing his song. He included several of his upward-gliding "cheeeeeeee"'s, which always serve to identify him. He was the only siskin we managed to record.

The river at Tres Ritos, in the Carson National Forest of northeastern New Mexico, was noisy, but we enjoyed revisiting old campsites of vacations in the thirties. A ruby-crowned kinglet song was our best souvenir from La Hunta Creek, above Tres Ritos. Another Townsend's solitaire looked us over, but this one wouldn't sing, either. We remembered how the dippers used to sing, often from a boulder in midstream near our old camp, but neither of the two we saw this time would sing. Dr. Kellogg got his dipper by placing a microphone on just such a midstream boulder, for which his bird had shown a preference. We found a dipper nest in plain sight on the side of a bare, vertical, shale bank where no predator without wings could reach it. The owner stood jiggling below for some time, blinking his white eyelid and *silently* speculating about our intentions.

Red River Canyon, where molybdenum, the rare metal used in steel alloys, is still being mined, showed much damage from erosion. The old wooden flume still carried water to the mine.

143

Down at Eagle Nest Lake we recorded a little western vesper sparrow, more meadowlarks, saw a solitaire, silent as usual. Near Taos we saw one prairie dog where we used to see scores. In Cimarron Canyon we recorded more western house wrens, a chipping sparrow, and a slightly different spotted towhee song, as well as the nesting vireo.

North of Walsenberg, Colorado, we stopped where a side road forded a rather serene little creek. Birds were flitting and twittering in the creosote brush along the fence. The twin Spanish Peaks rose in their solitude on the horizon to the south. Through the pasture east of us a boy of about ten or twelve, cantered on his calico pony. When we had explained to the olive-skinned Joey the purpose of our equipment, he waved his hand and suggested "wild canaries."

Here they were, two species of goldfinches only a few feet apart, the eastern and the black-backed variety of the "lesser," formerly known as the Arkansas goldfinch! No doubt the latter had been named for the river, not the state. We recorded the black-backed singer first because he was a "new species" for us—and our only recording of his kind, as time proved. The song of this "Arkansas" bore some resemblance to the vireolike song we had recorded from a green-backed (lesser) goldfinch near Tucson. But we heard none of the more typical goldfinch warbling from the black-backed bird. It's unhandy not having authorized common names for subspecies, which are easily distinguished in the field. After all, what are "common names" if not the names in common use?

After a magpie had talked for us in the Garden of the Gods, near Colorado Springs, our next recording stop was near Limon, Colorado. On these high prairies we found plenty of cooperative horned larks and soon lark buntings began to fill the meadows and wheat fields with their lively and distinctive songs. Lark buntings, black with large, white wing patches, are easily recognized in their breeding plumage, but a mottled wintering flock once had us puzzled for some time. I am all puffed up over the inclusion of my description of the song in Peterson's new Texas bird book. "Cardinal-like slurs, chat-like (unmusical) chugs, clear piping notes and trills, each note repeated three to eleven times." Much of their singing is done as they flit about the meadows in loose flocks. Fortunately for us they sometimes pause long enough to deliver a few songs from a fence post or a weed stalk.

In western Kansas we drove through a brief but black dust storm. We could see neither the road nor the front of our car yet continued to creep along both in fear of crashing into another car and in hope that we would soon get out of the path of the storm. With all car windows closed it was surprising how little dust got inside. At our motel that evening we met a man from the east who was still trembling from his experience. One of the sad things about such a storm is the way every resident tells you the dust is coming from some *other* part of the country, not his. The next day we encountered our first rain of the season. And the following night we had a hard time finding a place to sleep because the rain had caused a congestion of wheat-harvesting crews.

Are western birds more friendly than eastern? It seemed to us they were, but perhaps it was because we visited more sanctuaries and national parks on this trip. Another contributing factor toward that impression is the contrast in both songs and behavior between eastern and western meadowlarks. The eastern's songs are not only much high-pitched, weaker, and more pensive, but were usually delivered well back in the pasture—at least by the time we were ready to record. The western birds often stayed or came back to the telephone or fence post, next but one to our car, and continued their loud, lively, and varied cascades. One bird near Mesa had given us fourteen different song patterns within thirty minutes.

Approaching the region where eastern and western meadow-lark ranges meet we had wondered whether we would hear intermediate or hard-to-classify songs; none at all, at least along the route we followed we heard no hybrid songs. A certain upland meadow north of Belvedere, Kansas (near Dodge City), will be long remembered for the dawn chorus of western meadowlarks. A few miles east into Medicine Lodge River valley (near Lake City) we heard our first eastern meadow-lark, then no more from the western.

Near Sedan, Kansas, two upland plovers called their protests, but held to their territory as long as we did. They must have had a nest near. But they did not give the wild, siren-like cry we heard once, years ago near Dallas.

For sentiment's sake we recorded a cardinal at Indian Hill, near Erie, beside the old holiday cabin above the Neosho River, where Jerry began to study birds before he could read books.

The western bird population, like the human, is less dense than the eastern. Although we recorded about the same number of species in the same length of time, four months, as in the previous year, we had to drive 15,000 miles, an additional 5000. We exposed about ten miles or fifteen hours of tape, but, as usual, saved only about one fourth of it. We planned to record in the northwestern states the next year before making another LP record.

The winds blew us home on June 17—to find that our hundred-foot well had gone dry! We hauled water from a big spring, a half mile below us, for several weeks. No guests were invited that summer. We spent the time editing the tapes of our first western trip and keeping tabs on the birds at Avian Echoes.

[13] *Rosario Beach, on Puget Sound in Washington, was never so quiet again during our visit. Our first Puget Sound white crowned sparrow was recorded on the tilted log.*

[14] A mockingbird singing on the bank of the famous Suwanee River, here a broad but swift stream, was not to be resisted.

[15] *Swamp at Wakulla Springs, Florida, where the eerie screams of limpkins sent echoes through the woods. These rare, bronze wading birds are dependent for food on one species of large, fresh-water snail.*

[16] *Sunrise in Itaska State Park, near Park Rapids, Minnesota. The weird halloos of loons were recorded in this area.*

Chapter IX

SINGING STARS AND SNOWY VISTAS

WHILE visiting Harlingen again, in January and February of 1955, Jerry spent two weeks helping Irby Davis copy the best of his hundreds of Mexican bird recordings. Mrs. Davis couldn't listen as she had to meet her biology classes, but I was an enthusiastic kibitzer, scarcely willing to miss a note to put lunch on the table. How happy we were when Dr. Allen, after hearing a recital of Irby's recordings, said that Cornell Laboratory of Ornithology would like to sponsor the publication of a long-playing record of these Mexican songs!

During February we again haunted the two bird refuges which Luther Goldman, the director, had made more attractive than ever for the birds. The Valley mourned when he was transferred to Washington a few years later. Our best souvenir of the tropical Santa Ana tract that winter was the hoarse, whispered "screeps" of a barn owl. At Atascosa Refuge, predawn wildcat snarls were finally attributed to a Harris' hawk. (A year or two later we glimpsed a real wildcat at that very spot.) Geese, cranes, and curlews evaded us; curve-billed thrashers and pauraques were more obliging. A scattered "chorus" of horned owls called in different keys.

Arriving back at Avian Echoes on the official first day of spring, we were greeted with sleet and two inches of snow. We ignored this warning that spring would be three weeks later than normal in the northwest. Word reached us that prairie chickens were really talking around Pawhuska, Oklahoma. The birds were there; after much scouting we saw two flocks of about 100 birds each, but neither place gave us any chance of concealment. Then a smaller flock was found on another ranch; the stomping ground was in a pasture close to the house and outbuildings. With my reflector in the shadow of a barn, we finally caught their bagpiped "wooo-wooooos," "oh, ha ha has," henlike "clucks," "tut-tuts," and un-henlike "yeows." We recorded them without freezing any fingers or toes. Then the hospitable wife of the rancher invited us in for hot coffee and cakes, which, we surmised, she keeps on hand most of the time, not only for such wayfarers as us, but also for her school-aged grandchildren.

Sandhill cranes by tens of thousands foraged along the Platte River in Nebraska during the first week of April. They practically ignored us, partly, no doubt, because they felt safer in large flocks, but also because their courtship urge had begun and they were busy strutting, halooing, and doing their stately square dances. Their most typical call rises and falls like a siren, but has a rolling quality which may be approximated by vibrating the soft palate while imitating the call. We recorded so many that we heard "croo-oo-oos" in our dreams.

In a grove of cottonwoods near the river I caught the focus on a high, sweet, goldfinchlike song. But the bird was a drab sparrow color. When I finally saw the dark spot on his clear breast, as well as his rusty cap, we could hardly believe our luck. We caught the song of the only tree sparrow we ever heard sing! It was hard to refrain from thinking he had given his farewell song especially for us before taking off for his nesting grounds in Canada or Alaska.

Doris Gates, a friendly birder and biology instructor, introduced us to birds and birders about the city of North Platte. Prairie chickens were elusive, but we recorded the clamor of thousands of white-fronted geese on the river, and we broke our custom by taking a little unusual courtship talk from a pair of captive Canada geese in the city park.

Near Valentine, Nebraska, where pines and western meadowlarks begin, a kind field biologist jeeped our station wagon out of the worst mudholes while leading us to a roost of double-crested cormorants at one of the refuge lakes. The snaky-necked birds sounded like pigs grunting; unfortunately, their voices were almost drowned by wind and waves.

One morning our car bogged down in the muck at the edge of a lake on the Ballard Ranch. A two-mile walk to ask for help was welcome exercise because there was a skim of ice on the roadside puddles that April 15. When I had passed the cattle guard, still some distance from the ranch house, the cattle began to bawl, and retreat—except for a few with horns. Twice I withdrew to a mound within sight of rescuers. I waved and yelled, but was still so far away I couldn't tell whether the distant, moving figure was man or dog. At last I recognized a truck. The boy was just starting to school and had not seen or heard my signals. This thirteen-year-old boy handled a tractor as capably and confidently as a grownup in rescuing our car. This was the lake where we caught the long, descending wail of a pied-billed grebe. Plenty of horned larks and chestnut-collared longspurs were about, but doing little singing. However, we recorded fourteen song patterns from western meadowlarks in Nebraska.

South Dakota, from April 19 to 30, yielded a few more meadowlark songs and one weak, bantam squawk from a pheasant; he always crows as if he were being choked. We took a few snapshots of the Badlands and the scenic Black Hills. A patch of the big, fuzzy, lavender pasque flowers, or anemones, was almost the only sign of spring in the Black Hills. In sheltered ravines, we did see catkins of white birch and aspen, east meeting west. A dipper sang bravely but futilely above a rushing, ice-edged brook at Roughlock Picnic

Grounds. A snow shower the night before had laced and veiled all the pines and spruces above 4000 feet, to please photographers.

It rained both days as we traversed Montana, but south of Spokane we found spring at last, on the fifth of May. Cottonwoods and willows were leafing out, blue wild iris were abundant. Trout, or fawn, lilies, both creamy white and yellow varieties, were nodding. (Around Dallas, the first trout lilies, with white flowers and mottled leaves, usually open about February 5.)

Much of southeastern Washington is wheatland, often on slopes so steep we wondered how the tractors were prevented from tumbling downhill. Lavalike boulders are prominent in many pastures. Around the Turnbull Sanctuary, near Cheney, there are scattered pines and spruce. Here we followed the skyway circles of a winnowing Wilson's snipe until the mike line looked like a kitten's spool of thread. Several tule, or long-billed marsh wrens, chattered in the cattails, and went on record in spite of their nervous habit of popping in and out of sight—mike fright, no doubt.

No mike fright bothered the steely-blue little tree swallow at Sprague Lake. He came two or three times to the fence rail, just six feet from the reflector, opened his beak so wide his pink throat was in full view, and sang his very best. A few notes were musical, but his best was not very good and he had some competition from lapping wavelets and highway trucks. But he deserved an E for effort.

The highway along the south shore of the Columbia River, from Hood River to Portland, was at its scenic best on May 14. Here, dogwood blossoms, like many other flowers in Oregon, are larger than their eastern counterparts; they often have five flowery bracts instead of the four of the east. The wild, pink bleeding hearts are larger and deeper pink than Dutchman's breeches. Trilliums, anemones, and wild geraniums formed woodland carpets.

Southward, in meadows of the Willamette Valley, deep blue camas, or false hyacinth, were like pools reflecting the sky. Lupines of the west are often taller and of more varied hues than our Texas bluebonnets, also lupines, but rarely in such vast meadow and hillside carpets or of such a rich shade of blue. Along woodland margins we saw fuzzy-centered Mariposa lilies, often called pussy-ears, in pink or lavender or white. Pink wild roses, one kind with fringed petals, pink mallows, red columbine, "winecup" mallows bloomed near vine maples, which are really slender little trees. In Albany, Oregon dooryards, red-flowered hawthornes, small compact trees, were as prim and pretty as lace-frilled, colonial nosegays.

Our biggest recording day of the year was on May 23 when Kenneth and Virginia Gordon came along to help find and name the songsters, and to get some hints about bird recording. He was head of the biology department at Oregon State College in Corvallis. We recorded *twelve species* that day! It's hard to say which we appreciated more, the green-backed goldfinch or the turkey sandwiches. Virginia gets the credit for both.

Several recording sessions in McDonald Forest, a preserve belonging to the college, yielded a few warblers. We finally got the low notes of a sooty grouse, loud enough to be heard "if you stick your head 'way down in the horn."

One beautiful May morning we parked along a country road west of McDonald Forest. As we were unloading our equipment, a light truck approached from the south, then stopped in the middle of the narrow road about fifty feet before reaching us. It seemed a queer place to park, but we paid little attention until a car approached from the north and also parked in the middle of the road, thus blocking us. Then both drivers, dressed in rough clothes, got out of their cars and approached us on foot.

"This looks fishy to me," whispered Jerry, tucking his wallet out of sight in the car. Then he continued to unload the recorder and signaled to me to carry on as usual. I had brought out the reflector as the two burly men came near.

"Might an old-timer ask what you strangers are up to?" asked one.

Jerry laughed. "I was beginning to wonder the same thing about you."

"Scouting for uranium?" asked the second man. By this time close-up views had begun to dispel our mutual distrust. We just didn't look like Russian spies, and these farmers, who had obviously met by telephoned arrangement, did not act like holdup men. When we explained that we were trying to record bird songs, they apparently decided we were harmless freaks and soon left us in peace.

In the meantime, a faintly familiar bird song was coming from the thicket. Jerry spied him first—a lazuli bunting, one of our most-desired birds. His song somewhat resembles that of the indigo bunting; his light blue back, narrow, rusty breastband and white wing bars were easy marks of recognition. The three bird voices we treasured most, from the Willamette Valley, were the Puget Sound white-crowned sparrow, the lazuli bunting, and the green-backed (lesser) goldfinch.

When we crossed Santiam Pass, between Eugene and Bend, Oregon, on May 25, all the landscape, save the roadway, was still deep in snow. We heard our first varied thrush at the summit, but he was too far away to record. We went back to this very spot a month later and caught the song.

As we were going down the pass we came to a logging truck that the driver had deliberately ditched against an embankment. He realized it would be better to run into the bluff,

after his air brakes had suddenly sprung a leak, than to go over
one of the long drops on a hairpin curve. Luckily, his truck
was empty. We gave him a lift to the nearest telephone.

In the vicinity of Bend, on the eastern slopes of the Cascades, we had hoped to record sage grouse, but were too late
in the season for their talk. However, we did see a flock and
were surprised at their size, big as half-grown turkeys.

Deep in a pasture of sage and rabbit brush, we caught
a small colony of sage thrashers who, in spite of a snow flurry
the day before, May 26, were in a merry, singing mood. They
were very good singers, their melodies so long-continued that
we wondered when they caught their breath. They tinkled
along like musical toys that play as long as someone turns the
handle. The frequent recurrence of one accented note in the
song of one of the birds made him recognizable. We noticed
more individuality in the songs of this species than in other
thrashers. Although they perched at the tops of the sage
bushes to sing, their grayish backs and streaky breasts blended
so well with the foliage that the singers were hard to locate.

Malheur Refuge, near Burns, Oregon, with its shallow lakes
in a land of sagebrush, rocks, and scattered junipers, provided
a variety of birds. Poor-wills called before daylight. Wilson's
phalaropes swirled and dabbled. We taped the voices of willets, still more meadowlarks, long-billed curlews, a few crane
calls, superfluous after Nebraska's abundance, black terns and
yellow-headed blackbirds. These blackbirds walk like arthritic
old men, and talk like asthmatic ones.

While passing through the pine-clad John Day Mountains,
between Burns and Pendleton, we parked one morning near
the top of the divide. Our attention was first drawn by some
chatlike notes coming from a clump of bushes. Of course we
can't prove that a chat did not make them, but the bird we
saw fly out and waver up to the top of a pine tree was, of all
things, a *pine grosbeak!* Thick bill, rosy body and head,

153

prominent white wing bars on the blackish wings, robin size—all were noted. It was the only pine grosbeak we ever saw. The bird is quite rare in this country. He began to sing, a beautiful warble, more enchanting than that of the California purple finch! At the same moment a feisty little dog came dashing down the road from a cottage back in the woods, barking as if his owner's very life were at stake. And the bird flew away. We grieved over our only pine grosbeak.

May and June were spent alternating between Washington and Oregon. Washington has more stupendous, snow-clad scenery, but Oregon gave us more bird songs. Some of the finest scenery of our trip was along US 2 in north-central Washington. Lake Wenatchee, surrounded by snow-clad mountains, was worth the few miles detour just to see the deep, ultramarine blue of its waters. It seemed a deeper blue than either Tahoe or Crater Lake. Although Stevens Pass is only 4000 feet high, the landscape was deep in snow on the sixth of June. Several varied thrushes were heard, barely audible above the cataracts swollen by melting snow.

The bay at Rosario Beach, south of Anacortes in upper Puget Sound, was like a mirror the afternoon we arrived. We had not dreamed an ocean beach could be so quiet. In fact it was not as quiet again, during our short week's stay. Walla Walla College maintains a summer biological station at this location. We were guests of Dr. Ernest Booth, the director and also editor of a magazine called *The Naturalist*. Our cabin was only a few feet from the pebbled, log-strewn beach. One of the logs was the favorite singing perch of a Puget Sound white-crowned sparrow whose song we soon captured. The bluff on our right was a golden haze of Scotch broom. Beyond the projecting rocks, or "drowned mountains" in the bay, the Olympics formed a rugged horizon on clear days. Snow-capped Mount Baker was visible from the steep hill, called Mount Erie, back of the camp.

Halfway up Mount Baker the snowdrifts were higher than the car; again the long, quavering notes of varied thrushes were drowned. We began to think they would sing only to such accompaniment. We retreated from the mountain road with its deep snow and followed miles of dusty gravel to Baker Lake. It was off the beaten path for most tourists, and for its beautiful solitude we were glad to endure the slight inconveniences of a cabin with a kerosene lamp and an empty water bucket. A section of woods was found where both the brook and the breezes across the open lake were subdued. Here came the long, quavering notes! Each note has a different pitch, with a long pause between. Some are pleasing while others have a rough quality, as if two discordant pitches were sung at the same time. The song has an anthemlike quality which is characteristic of several of the thrush family.

Another winter wren was recorded at Baker Lake. It was our impression that winter wrens, Swainson's thrushes, long known in the east as olive-backed and in the west as the russet-backed, and olive-sided flycatchers were at least as common in the northwest as in the northeastern states. Robins also were prevalent and sounded to us just like the eastern variety, although we did not make a close study of them.

Giant conifers, fir, hemlock, western cedars, and spruce dominated the mountainous regions of western Washington and Oregon. One might have taken them for granted if there had not been conspicuous evidences of fire and lumbering devastation. "They" talk about selective cutting, but the cutover land we saw, especially in the Olympic peninsula, appeared to be completely ravished. The only hope against extinction of our big trees lies in the national parks and a few other reservations.

Rhododendrons, with their huge pink flowers, glowed even in the dense shade of the evergreens. Scotch broom quickly spreads a gilded mantle over many clearings. Madronas, usually slender trees, and Manzanitas, which are spreading shrubs, were seen in many woodlands. Both are members of the heath family, have thick, glossy leaves, lily-of-the-valley-shaped flowers, and conspicuous, rust-colored, smooth bark.

Along woodland paths the native Oregon holly-grapes bore tiny yellow flowers. This shrub, a Mahonia, adorns many Texas gardens. Red-flowered currants, yellow-flowered elderberries, and the magenta-pink raspberries, known as salmonberries, as well as another raspberry blossom of a species often called thimbleberry, with large, angular leaves and large white flowers, were all in bloom. Colonies of skunk cabbage were all dressed up in golden capes. This year, for the first time on many western visits, we found the corn lily, or false hellebore in bloom; the tall spikes of creamy flowers are showy, the large leaves resembling skunk cabbage. We had formerly assumed that it was some species of orchid.

Our circle trip around the Olympics was rather disappointing, as fog or showers hid the mountain peaks the entire three days. Side roads, so necessary to bird recording, were few and unproductive. Our best memento of the peninsula was another Puget Sound sparrow song. We had our best look at a sooty grouse, which sat so still we almost passed it by as a chunk of wood in the road; a few white spots were visible on his neck. Five band-tailed pigeons were heard and four seen. Three varied thrushes sang in the rain forest near Hoh River Ranger Station, but fog was dripping audibly from the moss-covered trees.

Rainier is undoubtedly the most beautiful mountain we have ever seen. Birds were rather scarce. The rangers lent us a key to a side road that was still closed to the public on account of snowdrifts. We drove two miles before the snow stopped us. We went up the road to Paradise Valley as far as the first glacier. Two varied thrushes sang, but one was out of reach and the other too close to a roaring stream.

We continued our trips between scenic Washington and, for us that year, bird-singing Oregon. In the Tygh Valley, southeast of Mount Hood, we recorded a few "screeps" and "zooms" from nighthawks early one morning. Along this road we saw our first Lewis woodpecker of the year, and another lazuli bunting, above a brook.

Near Bend, where Oregon pines grow 140 feet tall and three or four feet in diameter, and live 300 to 500 years, we tried one morning for a western bluebird—and got a good western fox sparrow. We luckily stopped in the center of his singing territory and thus were able to record him from several perches. In the cedarbrakes nearby we recorded a green-tailed towhee—almost as sweet.

On the road up to Crater Lake, elevation 7500 feet, I was not worried by the drop-offs because the snowdrifts were higher than the car in what might have been critical spots. The lake, surrounded by nearly vertical walls, was serenely blue and unapproachable, seeming not much closer than it does on a picture postcard. A Clark's nutcracker, the big, gray, sophisticated jay, foraged in a garbage can beside our car, but spoke not. A Cassin's finch, at the top of a towering spruce, was more cooperative.

Upper Klamath Lake, in Oregon, ranks high among the places we would like to go back to. The wooded mountains come down to meet the shore, but not too steeply. We actually saw a solitaire where there was room to park and traffic was light. We were ready to agree with the observers who declare that solitaires rarely sing in the spring, when other bird songsters are at their best. One black-headed grosbeak sang so well and so fast before full daylight one morning that we had our hopes up, for a little while, that he might be a solitaire.

Here western grebes were not shy but not very talkative, since parental duties had replaced courtship antics. Hermit thrushes, fox sparrows, and a ruby-crowned kinglet sang. We never could decide whether to nominate the western fox sparrow, black-headed grosbeak, or western meadowlark as "best in the west."

Lower Klamath Lake, just over the line in California, hadn't a bush or a weed to conceal us, yet we were lucky enough to get the calls of avocets and black-necked stilts, the clamor of California gulls, and calls of a few other species. As we recorded the voices of the stylish, slim, black-and-white stilts, they began to limp and flutter, trying to distract our attention from their half-grown children.

We drove into Lassen National Park and out again one morning before the ticket taker was up. The barren, volcanic slopes looked uninviting to would-be bird recorders.

Even on the map the US highway from Redding west to the California coast looked like a snake's trail, but it was the most feasible route for us. It began pretty well, a bit inclined toward hairpin curves, but the paving was wide and smooth and ran fairly close to the river. Then everything got steadily worse: narrower, sharper turns and steeper drop-offs, rougher, until we finally found ourselves, in late afternoon, the first car in an hour-long line, waiting for the road to be rebuilt in front of us. While some bulldozers were almost grazing our front bumper, others below were scraping the dirt out from under us until a mere inch or two saved us from rolling down the embankment. When we got the go-ahead signal the track in front of us was muddy and slippery, just wide enough for one car, yet two-way traffic was maintained, by occasional miracles. Then, to cap the climax—and the cliché fitted the situation only too well—in rolled the fog! We had to guess where the road was. The next day I bought some Dramamine pills.

In the coastal redwoods we were prevented from recording

a varied thrush and a winter wren by the logging trucks. Birds were especially scarce among the big trees.

At Point Lobos State Park, near Monterey, we found the Nuttall's white-crowned sparrows just where the park naturalist said they would be, and so tame we got recordings in spite of tourists and ocean waves. One bird ate cheese crackers and raisin cookies from my hand while Jerry fed the spotted ground squirrels the same way.

The Point Lobos white-crowned sparrow was the fourth subspecies we had recorded that year. Each subspecies, of the white-crowns we have recorded, had a different song, and all their songs in one neighborhood were approximately alike. But whether the range of a given song pattern *always* fits the nesting range of that subspecies we did not learn. With more thorough song collecting, we felt it *might* turn out that a given subspecies living in an isolated neighborhood would have a song differing from other members of his tribe.

We started back east.

A song sparrow bore sole honors for Nevada that year, a Brewer's sparrow for Idaho. The bare, desolate City of Rocks country south of Burley, Idaho, had a peculiar charm. One section, with nothing in sight to the far horizons but the smooth rocks of an old lava flow, gave us a feeling of being on top of the world; we imagined we could actually see the earth curving away in all directions. If we felt a little closer to heaven out there, it may have been because there was so little in sight on earth to hold or distract us. Farther down the road, among the boulders and a few bushes, we saw Brewer's sparrows and a green-tailed towhee, but the breezes were against us.

Road construction made it necessary to drop into Jackson's Hole via the famed, and fearfully remembered, Teton Pass. In fact it was worse than remembered, after fifteen years or so. The Grand Tetons, though, were just as grand as ever, the most rugged and majestic range we have ever seen. We met the young Hotchkisses here, and later at Homestead, Florida. He has since become a member of the Audubon Wildlife Films staff, as a naturalist-photographer-lecturer. They gave us some clues about where to look for birds, but we caught no new species here. We recorded another green-tailed towhee and a yellow warbler, but we only said "Fancy meeting you here!" to a catbird mewing from a willow thicket.

At Cheyenne Jerry suggested we turn north, not only to avoid the dust-bowl country, but as a last hope of adding new species to our western collection of songs. It was a lucky turn; south of Lusk we recorded McCown's and chestnut-collared longspurs, as well as more lark buntings to be compared with those from Colorado the previous summer. It was also good luck that we wandered off the main highway and thus found these vocal butterflies of the upland prairies. Of the four cars we met on this side road, two slowed down to avoid feeding us dust and the other two stopped to inquire if we needed any help.

McCown's and lark buntings have lively, tinkling songs in keeping with their flitting, carefree manners, habits reminiscent of bobolinks and Brewer's sparrows. The songs of McCown's longspurs are higher, thinner, and less varied in pitch and quality than those of lark buntings; pauses are frequent and irregular, and successive notes are not as repetitive as those of the buntings. Chestnut-collared longspurs sound like distant meadowlarks.

Back in Nebraska, calls of an upland plover were taped, still without the distinctive, long wails. Chatter from young, bronzed, yellow-headed blackbirds ended our recordings for the season. We reached our own rural Avian Echoes on July 20 and spent the next two months reviewing and filing the good parts of some eight miles of tape exposed that year. Including our preliminary, south Texas trip, we were away from home six months in 1955, traveled nearly 22,000 miles, and exposed forty reels, or ten hours, of tape. Although we recorded more than 300 times, only about 200 were worth saving.

Chapter X

THE BIRDS GIVE AN ENCORE

AT home, in 1956, after our second trip to the southwest, the porch was remodeled into a recording laboratory. One three-by-three cupboard was filled from floor to ceiling with bird tapes. We eventually catalogued more than 250 species of which some 164 were published on our three long-playing records.

The editing job for the western record was a big one. On the three western trips we had recorded 160 species of birds. To our surprise we managed to get sixty-eight of them on the record, with enough of each bird to show the characteristics of his songs. Many factors were considered in making the selections. Was the song recognizably different from his next-of-kin in the east? Was our recording adequate both as to quality and as representing the most *typical* songs or calls of the species? Was the song too high-pitched to transfer well onto a phonograph disc? Jerry always did the real editorial work, but I helped in making the selections. It took concentrated effort to get the tapes to the Fickers in Old Greenwich, Connecticut, by the date requested, choosing some 3300 feet of recorded tape from a stockpile of over 60,000 feet. There were not only the sixty-eight species to be chosen, but 138 individual birds and at least 223 *different* songs and calls.

Our first recording trip to a new section of the country always left us with gaps in our lists of much-wanted birds for that particular region, and we had often returned again and again, accumulating more reels of tape, and photographs, as souvenirs along the way.

With the western tapes edited, we had time to relax and play back recordings of southern bird songs and live over again the days we spent in the land of Spanish moss and wild turkeys. Our trips through Georgia and Florida had brought us several red-letter days and the capturing of much-wanted bird songs.

We had often made Thomasville, Georgia, our headquarters, taking drives from there into northern Florida. Our trailer park was located in a twenty-acre tract of natural woods. We wanted the owners to call it "Jouree Park" after the local name for the towhees; both wintering and resident varieties acted like members of the trailerite fraternity.

The country around Thomasville was much to our liking: gently rolling red hills, heavily timbered areas of both pine and hardwood, and many dignified, venerable, and stolid live oaks. There are many groves of pecans in this region, seemingly less tobacco than in Virginia, only small patches of scrawny cotton, but good sweet potatoes and some peanuts. A showy, yellow pea blossom covered fields and lined roadsides. We learned it is a Crotalaria, which is sometimes planted to enrich the soil. An abundant weed required a lot of page turning in the botanies, and then we were not pleased with the common names, dog fennel or Yankee weed. It has a faint, pleasant perfume, narrow leaves, and a long plume of feathery flowers.

On our first visit to Thomasville, in October of 1949, asters were scarce but goldenrod was plentiful. The dainty pink bells of Agalinis, or Gerardia, looked especially pretty hanging above patches of lavender mist flower, or wild ageratum.

Slender-stemmed coreopsis and other "yellow daisies" were in bloom.

Many of the autumn-flowering grasses conspicuous in this region were old friends of Dallas days. Especially prominent were the Andropogons, or beard grasses, from the tall turkey-foot, or big blue-stem, through the prairie beard grass to the lower silvery beard grasses. The coarsest one of the genus, bushy beard grass, likes lake margins and moist ditches. It took advantage of the ribbons of light along roads cut through densely forested swampy areas, sharing the roadsides with another which resembled Johnson grass but was taller and the heads longer, fuller, and more purplish. One morning we noticed especially the long, curving heads of Indian grass, their gold bright against the morning sun while lower grasses and weeds were still silver-spangled with dew.

We caught the best mockingbird song we ever heard in our trailer park at Thomasville. Jerry had hung a microphone in a dogwood tree and recorded the whisper song, which was barely audible at fifty feet. It continued for an hour, interrupted only when the singer was chasing marauding bluejays away from *his* dogwood berries. A day or so later, singing from an elm, he gave his full-voiced song and again the performance was taped. Forty years ago, Bradford Torrey wrote about the fine quality of the mockingbird songs in this region, as Maurice Thompson had done forty years before Torrey.

On another day we had taken our Kodak over to the famous Thomasville live oak. This venerable tree is said to be over 260 years old. It has a trunk circumference of twenty-one feet and the branches a spread of 152 feet. It is a natural monument, worthy of the respect and admiration it receives, and our photo of it is a cherished memento of our trip.

On a side trip from Thomasville, every mile from Carabelle through Apalachicola to Panama City had been a treat to us inlanders from the blackland prairies of Texas and we lived it again through our snapshots of the countryside. Pines and palms mingled along the beach. Cormorants were spread-eagled on stakes and stumps in the water, drying their dark plumage between plunges after finny prey. White terns sparkled in the blue sky. Big blue herons posed in the shallows and ospreys crowned dead treetops. Swallows skimmed the grass and a catbird mewed in a thicket. In the soft beach sand every hole was a shelter for side-scuttling little crabs, or for spiders and a variety of such small folk—a home for the first to arrive. We gathered a few stalks of seaside oats for winter bouquets. Oil willows were plentiful in the thickets, the many slender branches covered with tufts of white hairs to serve as parachutes for the seeds.

In north Florida US 90 has wide shoulders with graceful contours, draped not too regularly with crape myrtle and Pyracantha. The gently rolling terrain has pecan and tung groves, pine and hardwood plantations. The trees are similar to those in east Texas: sweet gum, tupelo, magnolia, live oak, red oak, laurel oak and sassafras above dogwood, French mulberry and sumac. Tulip trees, which lumbermen insist on calling yellow poplar, sometimes grow to immense size, are distinctive because of the big, v-shaped bite taken from the tips of the large, smooth leaves. The younger sweet gums had set their warning flares of starry, red leaves, but the older trees were not so easily alarmed by the first cool nights. There was only a scattering of deep red leaves among the green of the tupelos.

Among our souvenirs of another extended jaunt from Thomasville is a snapshot of the Suwannee River. We had eaten our lunch that day on the bank of the Foster-famed river, here a clear, broad stream, smooth-looking but with a swift current. A man was unloading his boatful of Spanish moss, gathered as mattress filling from branches overhanging the water. A mocker on the bank began to sing; he was not to

166

be resisted and we caught his song to remind us of the famous Suwannee.

On our first stop in Thomasville we had met Herbert Stoddard, formerly a member of the staff of the U. S. Fish and Wildlife Service. He was called, in those parts, "the quail man." Although Mr. Stoddard is well known for his many publications relating to wildlife, his most outstanding contribution was the result of his bobwhite study, a monumental treatise published in 1932.

Many predawn jaunts were made to the hospitable Stoddards' Sherwood plantation and we were indebted to him for helpful hints on where to find the local birds, particularly wild turkeys. They were relatively abundant in the region and we had expected no great difficulty in recording their calls. Stoddard's acre of goobers, in a far corner of his plantation, was a favored spot, but far from an electric outlet. We finally got the equipment set up in a neighbor's movie-shooting blind a dozen miles away.

Four mornings we tried there for turkeys, twice with a professional guide and turkey caller who scraped on a hollow block of wood and blew a tiny cowhorn, both homemade, imitating the voice of a hen turkey. Other birds sang but we caught no gobbles. Shortly after sunrise a big turkey strutted within ten feet of the mike, but not a gobble.

We wondered later, at home, why we tried so hard to record wild turkeys when none of the experts seem to detect any difference between the voices of the wild fowl and the barnyard bird.

One morning we heard a turkey gobble near one of Stoddard's tung groves. By noon we had stretched a wire nearly one-fourth mile from a power outlet in a barn to the shrubby border between the grove and a pine woods. About three o'clock next morning the recorder was set up—and there was no power. Jerry stumbled back along the line with a flashlight and, in a hollow, found that wood rats had chewed the rubber-coated wire into shreds in a dozen places. We spent the rest of the day repairing the damage, but before we left the plantation we discovered the favorite singing perch of a pinewoods sparrow in one of the tung trees. By the time we had secured a good sample of that sweet singer's repertoire, the turkeys had been forgiven and almost forgotten.

Although we had no tapes of turkey gobbles as souvenirs of those early-morning jaunts, one morning we caught something far more exciting, the calls of barred owls. With our equipment all set up for the turkeys that never cooperated, we waited for dawn and presently heard a barred owl call from a swamp a half-mile away. Jerry had an inspiration—he flashed the beam of our big electric lantern in the direction of the call, then into the tops of the pine trees nearby. The owls came over to see what was going on and repeated the standard barred-owl inquiry, "Who cooks for you?" while the recorder wheels revolved. The owls concluded their conversation with a final "whoo-all." Someone has said that the barred owl, the eight-hooter, when in Boston, says, "Who cooks for you? Who cooks for you?" but in the South says, "Who cooks for you-all?" At least one of our owls was a southerner. Before the owl concert was over a dawn chorus of daytime birds, including pine warblers, began to furnish a coloratura obbligato for the baritone owls.

The faint recordings of chuck-will's-widows, made at the Stoddard place, brought back memories of our repeated efforts to capture their songs. When Herbert Stoddard had told us that the chucks gave many odd calls in addition to their regular song we were especially anxious to record them. The chuck-will's-widow and the whippoorwill are close cousins and are similar in appearance although the whip is a little smaller. The latter is a northern bird, the first is southern, their breeding ranges overlapping, somewhat, along the Mason and Dixon line. Many people in the South are unaware of the differences and the bird they hear is often miscalled "whippoorwill." The names of the two birds give the best clue to the difference in their songs.

Morning after morning we tried for the chucks. One morning a bird would sing from shed "A"; next time the microphone at shed "A" would be useless because the bird sang from shed "B"; then we'd place the mike at shed "B" and the chuck would sing from shed "C"—or not at all. The voice of the chuck is heard on much of the tape we exposed there, but the recordings were too faint for use. The chuck-will's-widow used on our first published record was a regular summer resident of our Avian Echoes wood lot. He is also heard in the background of several of our Ozarkian bird songs.

The martins on our first LP record were taped at the Stoddard place. One morning we had noticed them chattering at a great rate. They lived in calabash gourd houses suspended from wooden crosspieces atop a twenty-foot pole in the front lawn. Jerry cut a long bamboo pole and hoisted the microphone to the middle of the calabashes. The martins' chatter was ten decibels above the noise of the wind and we were surprised at the musical quality of some of the martin talk. Their phrase "perfectly beautiful" *was* beautiful.

Reviewing taped favorites, we thrilled to the fervor of a white-eyed towhee we had recorded just outside Cypress Gardens in Florida. For five mornings we had parked our truck outside the garden fence, pulling the power line inside to a prearranged plug. Once there was wind. Twice it rained. Finally the weather was right and we found the favorite singing perch of the towhee in a low thicket. The bird came back within inches of where we had placed the microphone and gave us a stellar performance, a half-dozen variations of the familiar "drink tea" theme. He sang softly but with obvious fervor to convince his lady love that *this* clump, *this* bush, was the very best place to build her nest. Although it was a fine recording it did not find a place on any of our three LP records. The space was used for birds of wider territorial range.

The taped screams of limpkins brought back memories of the morning at Wakulla Springs, Florida, when we had shivered through three hours of predawn chill to record these rare wading birds. Jerry sat at the recorder, wrapped in a World War One blanket, with an electric light globe between his knees for added warmth, listening to and recording limpkins. They are chicken-sized birds, a white-speckled, dingy tan, turning to bronze in sunlight. At one time they were plentiful in Florida and rumors have it that early explorers sometimes were lost in the swamps searching for the "fair maidens" whose screams sounded like a woman being choked to death. The limpkin had other handicaps in addition to his harsh voice: he made a tasty dish whether spitted over the glowing coals of a camp fire or cooked in a pot. His only food is a large, fresh-water snail found only in the swamps; when Florida swamps were drained, both snails and limpkins became almost extinct.

One trip had taken us to Tampa in time to see an Audubon Wildlife Film program, where we met some of the local members. We not only saw the Pettingill pictures, but met Mrs. Leah Brownsey, a local naturalist who took us on several field trips. Since this was the wrong season for "singin' birds" we did most of our bird watching along the causeway across the bay between Tampa and Clearwater. Although we brought back no tapes, our snapshots refreshed our memories of the Florida shoreline.

Rows of Australian pines had been planted along the causeway as they are fast-growing and form a good windbreak. These trees which are *not* members of the pine family, look more like the athel trees of south Texas. The needles do not grow in bundles and they have tiny "joints" every half inch or so;

the seed cases resemble pine cones only in general shape and are about one-half inch long; the foliage is softer and fluffier-looking than that of the true pine.

Much of the shoreline of the causeway, and of many bays and inlets, is lined with a dense border of shrubby mangrove. Branches from the main stem spread downward into the mud, giving the appearance that root branches have been exposed by tides washing away the soil. Actually the reverse is true; these odd shrubs are helping to retain and build up the soil.

A rather rare and striking shrub of the beaches is called sea grape, for the grapelike fruits. The leaves are large, thick, stiff, circular, smooth, and red-veined, growing crowded and upright on the branches. It belongs to the knotweed family along with dock, buckwheat, smartweed, and rhubarb. Red veins seem to run in the family.

A highlight of one of our Florida trips was making the acquaintance of the late Charles Broley, who won world-wide fame for his work in banding eagles. Mrs. Broley's book, *The Eagle Man*, tells his heroic story. He was nearly seventy years of age, and since his retirement from a Canadian bank some ten years before, had devoted most of his time to observing, banding, and photographing our dwindling American emblem. A slight man, he was still able to climb eighty-foot pines via rope ladders—young men can't do it without first going into training—build blinds in treetops, and then, if necessary, stay up there three or four days in order to get motion pictures of nesting eagles in a nearby tree.

In Tampa Mr. Broley asked us if we had the calls of a bald eagle, and told us of a caged bird that we might record. Jerry said we were not interested in caged birds, but changed his mind after Broley said, "You may go quite awhile before you record that voice in the wild." We found the place and Mr. Rickard, the eagle owner, provided us with an electrical connection, even gave us pictures of the bird, and we got the calls after I approached the cage and flourished my cap. The eagle screamed in response. Broley had told us that the bird was a female; he recognized the sex by the difference in the calls. However, the bird, which was about twenty-eight years old, had always been called "Jim." The day before "he" died Jim laid an egg. Broley said, "Jim was a gentleman for twenty-eight years, then became a lady for one day."

Exploring near Bradenton one day, we saw two eagles. Jerry gave Mr. Broley minute directions for reaching the location. He merely smiled gently as he inquired, "And did you see the nest? It is about two hundred feet south of the culvert." That man knew his eagles. When we went back for a look at the nest only one eagle was seen in the neighborhood. A horned owl was perched on the nest and another owl nearby. We learned that someone had shot the eagle, alas, instead of the owl.

The beauty of the blooming Florida countryside around Tampa was enjoyed again as we pored over the snapshots we had taken along the way. In late December flowers were everywhere: scarlet turkscap, blooming since early fall, scarlet hibiscus, a few azaleas, purple draperies of bouganvilleas, gorgeous poinsettias, nasturtiums since Thanksgiving, petunias, snapdragons, calendulas, and acres of gladiolas out before the chrysanthemums were gone. To add to the flaming parade there had been cool nights to tint the sweet-gum and dogwood leaves while, in the same breath, the red maples were flaunting their scarlet spring keys. We found blue violets in bloom by the Hillsborough River on New Year's Day.

Elderberry bushes kept their green leaves, took no rest between fall fruits and spring flowers. There were Florida holly and the showy fruits of the bushy pepper trees. There were silk trees, "pink mimosa" to us folks from Texas, and another mimosa called "woman's tongue" because the foot-long pods were always rattling; blue-flowered jacarandas and golden-flowered silk oaks with silver-lined, ferny leaves—not resembling or related to the true oaks. The fluffy white catkins of bottle-brush trees began to open in early December. The tree's most striking characteristic is the bark, which is creamy-white and peels off in suedelike layers, hence the other name, punk tree. The scientific name, Melaleuca leucadendron, means black and white; it resembles eucalyptus and both are in the myrtle family along with cloves, allspice, and guavas.

Another day of reminiscence began with a snapshot of two long-time friends in front of their leaning live oaks in Rockport, Texas. Connie and Jack Hagar looked as young as ever and were busier than ever with bird watchers from everywhere. It would be hard to say whether the Anhinga Trail in the Everglades or the Hagars' place was the more popular gathering place of bird watchers. A few enjoyable days brought us no recordings. The gulf waves were not talking, but neither were the birds. One Inca dove did call near our cabin, but left before we could get ready for him.

Both bird-song tapes and Kodak books furnished abundant reminders of our two springs in the southwestern states and one in the northwest. One really rare prize was the successful recording of a Mearns's quail at Patagonia. At first we thought we were hearing a screech owl. He was on top of the low bluff, just out of sight. Then he flew down almost at our feet—his harlequin face was unmistakable. It was the only Mearns's quail we ever heard! Their trusting nature has given them the nickname of "fool quail." They are easily killed and have become very scarce.

The famous town of Tombstone stays in our memory as the place where we caught the talk of scaled quail. Along an abandoned highway through the pasture of a large ranch, we caught a covey of the "cottontops." These inconspicuous little gray "hens" with the white topknots are extremely shy; it was good luck that we were all ready to record and were standing motionless when the covey crossed our road. Apparently they did not notice us for they continued their chatter—"chuck-chuck, pur-ur"—and leisurely pace through the grass clumps, cacti, and low thorn bushes.

The tape of the black-throated sparrows at Tombstone brought back memories of my efforts to make myself invisible. The voices of these black-bibbed birds are so weak it is necessary to get quite close. I was on my knees in the gravel behind the reflector, trying to look like a cactus plant. One bird perched on a weed and sang several times within fifteen feet. This was the climax of a series of efforts for the species, beginning at Atascosa Refuge in Texas two years previously.

Our ten-day stay at the Southwestern Research Station of the American Museum of Natural History near Portal, Arizona, was the occasion for successful recordings of migrant redstarts from Mexico. Thanks to the guidance of Dr. Mont Cazier and his staff, we set up our equipment in the south fork of Cave Canyon. The brilliant, painted redstarts, red and black and white, were as fickle as butterflies, but singing closer to the ground than we had seen them before and, often enough, close to us. All we had to do was be patient, keep the recorder running, and try to guess which one of the half-dozen birds would sing next—and when—and where. Now it would be from an oak branch overhead, next a boulder on the other side of the roadway, sometimes from the road itself. Often we got only a note or two at a time, but gradually the songs were taped. Playing them now, it seemed to us that these beautiful immigrants from Mexico were sweeter and more versatile singers than the redstarts of the eastern states.

The antiphonal trio of Cassin's kingbirds on our western record came from a tall cottonwood shading the Caziers' residence. A tiny, charming, bridled titmouse sang his best for us, but lost his place to more musical and more widespread species.

Catching the weak song of a phainopepla, near Mesa, had been another of our red-letter days. We had gone out to Coon Bluff Picnic Ground in the hope of avoiding wind and traffic. Out in the mesquite section we had just finished recording another Lucy's warbler when we spotted a singing phainopepla. His song is, at best, a rather weak, broken warble, hardly worthy of such a handsome, black-taffeta-coated aristocrat who holds his crest so high. I turned the reflector this way and that as he kept on singing. At last Jerry said, "Hold it!" and soon we had the song of the best phainopepla singer we ever heard. Hearing it again, in the quiet of our home, brought a thrill of satisfaction.

Near Tucson, on our second trip to the southwest, our first songs of Scott's orioles were recorded near the Sonora Desert Museum—successfully, at a distance of 200 feet! These orioles, which often prefer yuccas for nesting and song perches, have loud, full voices and each individual seems to have his own tune, as Baltimores do. They really lived up to their reputation and were by far our most musical new species for the year 1956. Later that summer we recorded six or eight more Scott's orioles, whereas we had merely seen one in 1954. In two short visits to Ramsey Canyon, south of Fort Huachuca (the civilian village is called Fry), we taped our nearest Scott's oriole in a sycamore only twenty-five feet away. This is the best of the several songs of the species on our western record.

Soon after our first orioles had moved on from our location near the museum headquarters, a bunch of Brewer's sparrows drifted in like thistledown, though usually inclined to scatter on even less provocation. However, as the nesting season draws near, they are more apt to ignore human interlopers. We had exceptional success in recording the species on this occasion. Then for good measure of good luck that same day, we got the dawn song of Say's phoebe and a new type of "song" from a cactus wren!

Madera Canyon, south of Tucson, had lived up to the recommendations of Erle Morton. Here were new and interesting birds miles away from heavy traffic. The stream was large enough to attract birds and small enough not to be noisy. Live oaks, sycamores, juniper, and pines surrounded our cabin. One morning a Steller's jay and two acorn woodpeckers frolicked through the big live oak shading our roof. Both species can be loquacious and they used their full vocabularies. The stylized Steller's jay on the jacket of our western record earned his place of honor at Madera Canyon.

Near Kerrville, Texas, after miles of gray sage, we welcomed the green cedarbrakes. Arkansas goldfinches were flitting along the valley roads. Such songs as we heard from them sounded like the one we had recorded near Walsenberg two years earlier —only the leisurely couplets and slurs, none of the rapid warbles typical of other goldfinches. Has anyone heard the black-backed variety of the lesser goldfinch give a warbling song? If so, Dr. Wendell Taber, who is completing the Bent series of *Life Histories of Birds*, would be glad to hear about it. Since the green-backed variety has two types of song, it seems reasonable that the black-backs may also have two.

Oddly enough, our best Cassin's sparrow recording is a souvenir of a trip through Dallas, rather than the Valley, where they are much more plentiful. In the southwestern outskirts of the city, near Mountain Creek Lake, we found the bird singing, and, lucky for us, about half the time he sang from a fence post instead of in the air. Each Cassin's sparrow we have heard sings a plaintive little trill followed by two lower and shorter notes, repeating the refrain in just two keys, sung alternately. We did not hear the low opening notes mentioned in Peterson's guide.

We also caught the dry, staccato chatter of a black-capped

vireo not far from the Cassin's sparrow that morning. We were sorry to have to leave both birds off our western record, crowded out by species of wider distribution.

Having records of nesting birds, migrating species, and winter residents in different parts of the country gave us an opportunity to study songs under varying conditons and circumstances. As we edited our tapes and evaluated the songs recorded we found the answers to some of the more frequently asked questions.

During a casual conversation with a bird beginner we had been asked if female birds ever sing. The answer is a definite yes, as far as cardinals and at least a few other species are concerned, although the female cardinals we have heard joined in only the simpler songs. There was no way for us to know whether the blue-headed vireo which warbled from the nest at Mountain Lake, Virginia, was male or female; the sexes look quite alike and it is known that the male of the species often takes his turn in sitting on the nest, which is not the case with many birds. For example, the male dickcissel, a member of the sparrow family, is said never to go near the nest, seeming to feel that his full duty to his family has been covered when he sings his simple ditty. He works most assiduously at repeating "Dick! Dick! Sis, sis, sis."

Another question sometimes asked is, "Why do birds sing?" Several thousand dollars were recently donated by a large trust fund to certain ornithologists who are making a special, scientific study of the question. It is now generally believed that a majority of bird songs are territorial in purpose, granting a double objective of attracting a possible mate, as well as warning away rivals.

The brave curve-billed thrasher in Sabino Canyon, near Tucson, the little tree swallow at Sprague Lake in Washington, the blue-headed vireo at Mountain Lake in Virginia, possibly the barred owls near Thomasville, the rock wren in the canyon north of Big Bear Lake in California, the "Arkansas" goldfinch near Walsenberg, Colorado, the fox sparrow near Santiam Pass in Oregon—all are memorable examples of birds which were not only exhibiting territorialism, but were warning *us* to please get out of their nesting territory. Since birds which have established their territory and favorite singing perches are much easier to record than the more unpredictable ones, it is probable that a great majority of the songs we recorded should be called territorial.

A few bird songs are unmistakably special courtship recitals. They seem to be rare and usually of low volume. We have recorded only one we are positive belongs in this class, the white-eyed towhee at Cypress Gardens in Florida. A different-from-usual and less musical flight song of an eastern meadowlark that we recorded may possibly be a courtship song, but we were not sure; it is weaker than his other songs and shorter. We treasured the memory of a cardinal courtship song which we heard in Dallas before our recording days. It was soft, beautiful, and fervent, very different from usual cardinal songs —and successful! And Jerry once heard a special courtship song from a chat at Avian Echoes.

Interest has also been expressed in the purpose of flock singing. It may serve to keep a group of one species together, through vocal recognition, although many birds, such as geese, ducks, blackbirds, and bobwhites usually accomplish this by special calls which could not be classified as songs. Birds which sing in flocks during migration include some of the thrushes, orioles, goldfinches, pine siskins, and white-crowned sparrows; the latter also do quite a bit of winter singing as do whitethroats and fox sparrows. Goldfinches often continue their flock singing after migration is finished and before nesting has begun. Others, such as lark buntings, longspurs, horned larks, Brewer's sparrows, and bobolinks seem to continue flock singing into the nesting period, for reasons not yet known.

Some birds sing different songs at different hours, such as the more elaborate dawn songs of pewees and many other fly-catchers. Some listeners believe the night songs of mocking-birds, chats, and others are different from their daytime songs, but the imagination of the listener may be a factor here. Often there are different songs at different seasons. There is doubt as to the purpose of whisper songs, often heard in late summer; some may be practice songs of young birds. And the purpose of fall and winter songs remains a mystery.

We conclude that there are some bird songs that cannot be territorial, courtship, or flock recognition. According to Aretas Saunders, "Many songs serve no biological purpose whatso-ever." We are neither so sentimental nor so egotistical as to really believe that birds ever sing to please people. If the reader has noticed herein that a certain bird "sang for us," it was not meant to be taken literally. But may it not be that, at least once in a while, birds do sing for the same reason that humans sing in the bathtub—because they enjoy the sound of their own voices, in other words, just for fun?

After the publication of our western record, we had begun again our efforts to collect more voices of water and game birds. Our tape of the long, thrilling halloos of upland plovers, recorded near Spirit Lake, Iowa, started recollections of our trip to the north lake country, beginning in mid-June of 1957. The plover whoops were not as loud as we had expected, per-haps because it was near the end of their nesting season. We had recorded only their scolding notes in previous years.

Although the plover is often seen in the Dallas region dur-ing migration, we had heard its long, siren cry here only once, years ago, in a low meadow of the Trinity Valley, just north of the city. Jerry recognized the weird call and it brought memories of boyhood days. These "courtship flight songs" are best described by quotations from Bent's *Life Histories of North American Shore Birds*, bulletin 146 of the U. S. National Museum. Bent quotes Fred J. Pierce:

Their shrill, penetrating whistle will carry nearly a mile, depending upon the wind and the altitude of the whistler. First there are a few notes sounding like water gurgling from a large bottle, then comes the loud *whip-whee-ee-you*, long drawn out and weirdly thrilling.

And, condensed from Professor Lynd Jones in the same bulletin:

The first part of the whistle, usually trilled, passes upward nearly an octave, then gradually falling again and decreasing in volume to the close, several tones above the beginning.

The prairie lakes of the Dakotas gave us fine views of water birds but their more vocal courtship season was over. Our best tape souvenirs were the mud-sucking sound "oong-a-lunk" of an American bittern, chatter from avocets, and a marbled godwit and a good recording of the weak, buzzy trills of a clay-colored sparrow.

We stopped at Park Rapids, Minnesota, in real northwoods lake country where there are hundreds of lovely little lakes edged with pines and hemlocks and white-barked birches. At Mary's Lake, in Itasca State Park, we found loons in vocal mood. This body of water is so small that it was no great handicap to have the loud-voiced birds close to the far shore. We happily registered their tremolos, uncanny laughter, and crescendo yodels and heard them again now with nostalgia. New song patterns from several Baltimore orioles and a few white-throated sparrow anthems were further mementoes of the region.

Near Thief River Falls, Minnesota, we caught the clamor of a flock of Franklin's gulls. The Kodak book recorded lakes from Ely, Minnesota, to and along the shore of Lake Superior as well as delightfully isolated lakes of northern Wisconsin.

In 1958 we again revisited southern Texas, Arizona, and California. We secured no new species that year, but obtained improved examples of the vocalizations of coots, pied-billed grebes, kingfishers and Inca doves.

The spring of 1959 was spent along the Atlantic coast from Georgia all the way to Maine. At St. Simon's Island and its twin, Jekyll Island, we found the greatest concentration of wading and shore birds we had ever seen—thousands of them —and none talking! Ospreys at St. Simon's looked down on us from their nests, but we had no Allan Cruickshank, the famous bird photographer, to climb the tree and make them scream.

Near New Bern, North Carolina, out on Cedar Island, we managed to record a few calls of laughing gulls, failed to catch a least tern, and some interesting talk from a pair of gannets, which flew by with a sound like wheels creaking.

From Nags Head to Cape Hatteras, a billow-tossed beach threw sand at us until we were coated from head to foot with a fine, sticky, gritty layer.

At the Hilltop Cabins in Plymouth we recorded a Baltimore oriole, with a new song, of course, as every Baltimore has his own tune. On Cape Cod we found the most birds out near the tip, where scrub pines and wild plums are making a valiant effort to pin down the sand dunes. On this part of the cape, near Provincetown, summer homes had not completely monopolized the land. The few shore birds were wary and silent.

The most exquisite sight on scenic Mount Desert Island, in Acadian National Park, and facing Northeast Harbour, was a garden all glowing with pink, from pink-flowered dogwood down to edgings of pink phlox and oxalis.

In Maine neither Pemaquid Point nor Belfast Bay yielded any birds. We consoled ourselves with a real, down-east, boiled-lobster picnic on the beach at Belfast. Chilly, but fun.

The scenery was wonderful along the Atlantic, but the shore birds we had hoped for failed to cooperate. At last it became clear that our dream of a record of water and game birds was not to be, for us. Younger recorders now scout the shores and crouch in the bulrushes.

Twelve strenuous but happy springs of recording bird songs! More than 180,000 leisurely miles along country byways. Three long-playing records published! Memories of the finest scenery in all the country, and many out-of-the-way places not found by tourists who follow only the main highways. Numerous friendly folks along the way. Many congenial birders. And new friends via microgroove! Letters from strangers who had heard our records. Some of the letters gave glimpses of the writers' life stories, of their personalities or their own viewpoints on our mutual interest in birds. One woman wrote about her years of birding in Mexico and in Hawaii. We received many invitations to come to somebody's favorite retreat and record his favorite birds. A songwriter, 104 years of age, proposed a record of barnyard sounds, and offered very canny suggestions on ways to get the animals to produce certain desired sounds. One especially generous microgroove friend wrote:

Your record transformed our winter day into spring. When we heard the brown thrasher we were magically transported from a day in February to that damp, burgeoning day in April when, from the top of a cottonwood tree out in our nearby forest preserve, he gives us his first glad concert of his season. As the field sparrow contributed his portion of the medley we were borne as upon a magic carpet to brushy pastures bedecked with red clover and we could almost smell the hot, dusty atmosphere of a midsummer day whose heat seems never too great to daunt the spirit of this persistent little songster. . . . In having your fun you are also bringing great pleasure to people like ourselves, who, though completely unknown to you, are nevertheless amateur members of your fraternity.

INDEX

Cabbage palms, 63
Cactus wrens, 21–22, 29, 132, 176
Cadillac, Mich., 40, 41
California, 135–41, 158–59, 181
California gulls, 158
California purple finches, 140
California scrub jays, 138
Callicarpa, 53
Camerons' antique shop, 85
Camp Ellowi, 64, 101
Canada geese, 128, 129, 149
Canada warblers, 114
Canyon towhees, 138
Canyon wrens, 33, 131
Cape Cod, Mass., 181
Cape Sable sparrows, 59, 60
Carambolas, 64
Cardinals, 3, 6–7, 9, 30–31, 58, 81, 95, 96, 99, 101, 146, 177, 178; Arizona, 134; bullfinch, 21; Kentucky, 7
Carlisle, Pa., 46
Carolina chickadees, 7
Carolina wrens, 9, 81, 94, 96, 100, 101
Carruthers, Vera, 44
Carson Natl. Forest, 143
Cassin's finches, 140, 157
Cassin's kingbirds, 174
Cassin's sparrows, 24, 130, 176
Catbirds, 79, 95, 160
Cater, M. B., 108
Cave Canyon, 174
Cazier, Mont, 174
Cedar Island, 181
Cedar waxwings, 110
Cerulean warblers, 108
Chacahoula, La., 128
Chachalacas, 26, 29, 114
Chagrin Falls, Ohio, 44, 45
Chalmette, La., 127
Charlottesville, Va., 49

Chats, 79, 91–92, 101, 139, 178, 179
Chestnut-collared longspurs, 116, 149
Chestnut-sided warblers, 110
Chicago, Ill., 34
Chickadees, 7, 97, 114, 121, 138–39, 140
Chipping sparrows, 40, 77–78, 97, 144
Cholly, Mr. and Mrs., 59–60
Chuck-will's-widows, 114, 168–69
Cimarron Canyon, 142, 144
City of Rocks (Idaho), 159
Clark's nutcrackers, 157
Clark's Service Station, 49–50
Clarksville, Tenn., 83
Clarksville, Va., 50
Clay-colored sparrows, 180
Cleveland, Ohio, 43, 44
Coffey, Mr. and Mrs. Ben, 108, 126
Colorado, 144
Columbia River, 150
Comstock, Anna Botsford, 67
Cook, Clarence D., 36–38
Coon Bluff Picnic Grounds, 134, 175
Coots, 57, 133, 181
Coralbean, 63
Cormorants, 149, 166
Cornell Univ., xii, 7, 31, 56, 67–68, 122, 125, 147
Corn lily, 156
Couch, Mrs., 111
Couch's kingbird, 24, 26–27
Courtship songs, 178
Cranes, 60, 148, 153
Cranesville Bog, 114
Crater Lake, 157
Crawdads, 127
Crested flycatchers, 9, 25, 27, 29
Crotalaria, 164

The Stillwell's Favorite Areas
for Recording Bird Songs

① ② etc.—See pages XVII, XVIII, XIX for key listing
areas and typical birds